THE NEW ILLUSTRATED GUIDE TO

MODERN AMERICAN FIGHTERS
& ATTACK AIRCRAFT

SMITHMARK

——— THE NEW ILLUSTRATED GUIDE TO ———

MODERN AMERICAN
FIGHTERS
& ATTACK AIRCRAFT

MIKE SPICK & BARRY WHEELER

A Salamander Book

©Salamander Books Ltd.,

This edition published in 1992 by
SMITHMARK Publishers, Inc.,
16 East 32nd Street, New York,
NY 10016,
(212) 532-6600.

ISBN 0-8317-5059-6

Credits

Authors: Barry Wheeler is a writer and defense journalist who is currently the editor of *Air International* magazine. Mike Spick is a freelance writer who specializes in aviation subjects.

Editor: Graham Smith
Designer: Mark Holt
Filmset by: The Old Mill, London.
Color Reproduction: by Scantrans PTE, Singapore.
Printed in Singapore

Acknowledgements

The publishers wish to thank the many individuals, especially those in the US government, armed services and aerospace industry who have helped with the provision of photographs for this book.

Contents

Introduction

ANY review of American combat aircraft is inextricably linked with the operating arms, and in the case of the USA this involves four major organisations—the US Air Force, the US Navy, the US Marine Corps, and US Army Aviation. Together they operate or have requirements for nearly 27,000 aircraft; the largest number of military aeroplanes and helicopters used by any single nation.

The US Air Force was established in 1947 from the US Army Air Force, and is today the most powerful single military arm in the USA (and indeed, in the Western World). Until 1992 the USAF comprised some twelve different commands, of which just two were principal front line formations — Strategic Air Command, with headquarters at Offut AFB, Nebraska, and Tactical Air Command, embracing Air Defense TAC (AD-TAC) at Langley AFB, Virginia. In addition there were TAC-assigned units in the Air Force Reserve and the Air National Guard. In September 1991 a comprehensive restructuring was announced where all fighters, bombers and reconnaissance aircraft would come under the control of Air Combat Command (ACC). Transport and tanker aircraft would be controlled by Air Mobility Command (AMC), although the two overseas commands, PACAF (US Pacific Air Forces) and USAFE (US Air Forces Europe), would retain control of all assets in their respective theatres.

While the user commands are the final link in the evolutionary chain which produces American combat aircraft, there are other elements in between, one of the most important being Air Force Systems Command, which evaluates the aircraft or weapons required by the operator; a successful evaluation may result in AFSC placing a contract with the manufacturer.

Restructuring

The makeup and posture of the armed forces of any nation are essentially a response to a real or potential threat. From a

Below: Like a sinister black science fiction creature, an F-117A stealth fighter sits in a Saudi hardened shelter during the Gulf War.

Above: This prototype E-8 J-STARS radar system can track and identify ground targets over an area of hundreds of square miles.

Western perspective, the major threat to world peace over the past four decades has traditionally come from the Soviet Union. During this time, Strategic Air Command held the ring for the USA, controlling the ICBM and manned bomber forces; the third leg of the nuclear triad deterrent being the US Navy's missile submarines.

In late 1991, SAC operated some 261 B-52G/H Stratofortresses and 96 B-1B Lancers. The majority of the former were over twenty years old, and it had been planned that most of the G models would be retired during

the mid '90s, leaving the turbofan powered B-52Hs to soldier on as cruise missile carriers in the stand-off role. The penetration role was to be filled solely by the B-1B, which in spite of a bad press, is far more capable than is often acknowledged. With the planned service entry of the B-2A stealth bomber in the second half of the decade, the B-1 would then have reverted to the stand-off role as a primary mission.

Other aircraft operated by SAC were a large fleet of tankers, KC-135s and KC-10As, for in-flight refuelling. The FB-111 low-

Below: In-flight refuelling is an essential force-multiplier for US forces; this Air Force KC-135 is topping up a Navy EA-6 Prowler.

Above: The US Navy carrier groups have provided unique global reach, but 1990s defence cuts are reducing the size of the force.

level penetrators had been withdrawn from SAC in 1990/91 to be modified as F-111Gs and reissued to TAC.

Events in the Soviet Union from 1988 onward, culminating in the dissolution of that body at the end of 1991, diminished the intensity of the threat and radically altered its nature. Down the years, about one third of the B-52 and B-1B force had stood alert, armed and ready to go; with tankers standing ready to support them. Then in September 1991, alert status was reduced, while a massive reduction in American nuclear weapons was announced.

Even before this it had become obvious that the diminished threat no longer justified the existing defensive posture, while SAC aircraft were being allocated an ever increasing number of tactical rather than strategic missions. Far reaching changes were put in hand. Before these could be implemented, they were modified still further by lessons learned during the Gulf crisis. Operation Desert Shield in the final quarter of 1990, followed by Desert Storm early in the following year, showed that greater flexibility was needed.

A further reason for radical restructuring was economic difficulty within the USA. As the Soviet threat receded, so calls for the 'peace dividend', a reduction in defence spending with the savings arising going to what were seen as more worthy causes, multiplied. A case for a dedicated strategic nuclear bomber force could no longer realistically be made, and the search was on to find better ways of doing more with less in the tactical field.

As noted earlier, this was achieved by revamping the entire Air Force command structure. SAC was dissolved and its assets redistributed. The ICBM force was put totally under joint interservice command, which had always been fairly much the case in any event; while its combat aircraft were taken over by TAC to form ACC. The tanker fleet became part of the new AMC, joining the transport fleet previously belonging to Military Airlift Command (MAC), which was also dissolved. Both ACC and AMC officially came into being on 1 January 1992. At field level, the need for force packages was identified. Traditionally, a mission had been put together

Above: The Marines see VSTOL aircraft (such as this AV-8B) as a means of providing support to ground troops without the Navy's supercarriers.

using various aircraft types, typically attack aircraft with fighter escorts, EW aircraft and Wild Weasels and tankers. All except tankers now come under ACC, which makes it much easier to put together and co-ordinate a composite force able to operate autonomously from its own resources.

The Manned Bomber Force

Now a component of ACC, the manned bomber units are operated by 8th and 15th Air Forces, and currently consist of ten B-52 Wings and four B-1B Wings. Generally considered incapable of penetrating a modern air defence system, even with the aid of massive counter-

Below: The B-1 Lancer has been plagued by technical problems, although few doubt its ability to do its job in wartime conditions.

measure support, prime mission of the huge eight-engined B-52 is that of a stand-off missile carrier in the nuclear deterrent role. The 'Buff' also acts as a classic heavy bomber in tactical warfare, carrying an awesome load of conventional ordnance to saturate an area.

The four B-1B Wings, based at Dyess, Ellsworth, Grand Forks and McConnell air bases, carry the burden of deep penetration at low level, but they can also tote a considerable load of conventional ordnance, including sea mines. It has often been stated that the B-1B is no longer viable in the penetration role against the Soviet (or Russian) air defence system, but to what degree this is fact, and to what extent it is propoganda put out to ease the entry into service of the B-2A, is difficult to judge. Certainly the Lancer would be effective against any other possible adversary.

After years of speculation, the Northrop B-2A was finally revealed as a flying wing of moderate sweep and fairly high aspect ratio, with no vertical surfaces. Intended to penetrate hostile airspace undetected, at medium to high altitudes and subsonic speeds, it is optimised for low observability. While the original requirement was for 132 aircraft, this has since been cut to 75, and in January 1992, the decision to fund only fifteen of these aircraft was announced. It is highly unlikely that any more will be built, so for the foreseeable future the B-1B will retain the role of low level penetrator while taking over some of the tactical tasks of the antediluvian B-52.

Tactical Aircraft

Another effect of defence cuts is a general reduction in force levels, with various units being deactivated, others being relocated, and bases being closed both at home and abroad. Thirty-five tactical fighter wings are currently active; the original target of 40 will not now be achieved, and the final number is expected to be 34; a far cry from the 143 wings projected in the early '50s. But even as numbers reduce, re-equipment with new aircraft still proceeds, although at a more leisurely pace than hitherto.

The A-7D/K Corsair II is now flown exclusively by the ANG, while the four remaining squadrons of F-4E Phantom IIs are operated by AF Reserve (AFRes) units. The Phantom is

Below: The B-2 Stealth bomber was planned to replace the B-1 and B-52, although it now seems as if only token numbers will see service.

Above: Still soldiering on, the veteran Phantom has found a new lease of life in the 'Wild Weasel' defence suppression role as the F-4G.

now into its fourth decade and long overdue for retirement, and the RF-4C reconnaissance variant will be phased out in favour of the ATARS equipped RF-16C commencing in 1993. This leaves the F-4G Wild Weasel defence suppression aircraft to be replaced. The main candidate is the F-15E. The Panavia Tornado has been mooted for the role, but acquisition of a foreign aircraft is hardly likely, given the depressed state of the US defense industry.

The F-15C/D is the backbone of the air superiority units, although a few units retain the more spritely but less capable F-15A/B. The most recent member of the family is the F-15E Strike Eagle which entered service in December 1988. A two-seater interdiction aircraft with tremendous load carrying capability, it is fully agile once it has expended its air-to-surface ordnance and can double in the air superiority role. In all, approximately 420 F-15A/Bs and 460 F-15C/Ds are in service, with procurement of Strike Eagles limited to 200 (against an original requirement of 392).

The F-16, originally conceived as an agile light fighter, is now

Below: A-10s and F-16s currently form the backbone of the Air Force's CAS (Close Air Support) and BAI (Battlefield Air Interdiction) force.

Above: The 'E' model of the original F-15 Eagle air superiority aircraft has been developed into a superb multi-role strike fighter.

Above: The future USAF fighter, the F-22. Stealth, vectored thrust and supersonic cruise should give it the edge over any opponent.

equipped as a multirole aircraft used for both air combat and the ground attack mission. Some 2,459 have been committed to date, 785 of them A/B versions, plus 26 F-16Ns for the US Navy. Production is scheduled to end in 1999. The latest Block 40 aircraft have more powerful GE or P&W turbofans, restoring the thrust/weight ratio and performance, if not quite the agility, of the A model. In October 1986, the F-16A was also selected for the continental air defence mission. Equipped with modified radar and carrying AIM-7 Sparrow or AIM-120 AMRAAM missiles, this variant is used by ten ANG squadrons tasked with air defence. It now appears that

the F-16 will take over the close air support/battlefield air interdiction mission from the A-10A, while as mentioned earlier, the RF-16C will replace the elderly RF-4C in the near future. In the Wild Weasel replacement contest, the two seater F-16 has not been ruled out. It is also possible that a much modified F-16 variant will be offered as an F-16 replacement towards the end of the '90s.

The F-16 was the final mount of the rather exotic Aggressor squadrons, which have now been deactivated. Economy was the main reason given, but another underlying reason was that the original *raison d'etre*, dissimilar air combat, had been

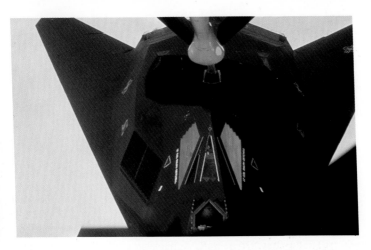

Above: The first generation Stealth aircraft, the F-117A, is seen here refuelling on its deployment to the Gulf in 1991.

lost with the service entry of the Russian MiG-29 Fulcrum and Sukhoi Su-27 Flanker. These superb aircraft have performance characteristics similar to the F-16 and F-15 respectively. In effect, dissimilar air combat can now be carried out between units operating the F-16 and F-15.

July 1992 saw the 20th anniversary of the first flight of the F-15 prototype, and while the Eagle remains arguably the world's best air superiority fighter, the basic concept is over 30 years old. The F-15 is to be superseded by the Advanced Tactical Fighter (ATF) which combines supercruise (the ability to cruise at supersonic speeds) with advanced manoeuvrability and a significant number of low observability features. After a flight evaluation of the two contenders, the Northrop/McDonnell Douglas YF-23A and the Lockheed/General Dynamics/Boeing YF-22A, the latter was selected for further development and production, with Initial Operational Capability (IOC) scheduled for 2002. At the time of writing, 570 F-22As and 80 two seater F-22Bs are required, but whether this is adhered to depends on both world affairs and economic factors.

Looking to the future, the MBB/Rockwell X-31A Enhanced Fighter Manoeuvrability aircraft is undergoing trials to examine the combat value of post-stall manoeuvring. A small, single engined canard delta with thrust vectoring paddles, two X-31As have been built specifically for these trials. The post-stall flight envelope is larger than is often realised. For example, a stall speed of 150kt (278km/hr) at sea level becomes nearly 300kt (556km/hr) in the thin air at 40,000ft (12,191m). Wind on a modest 4g turn, and this doubles once again to nearly 600kt (1,112km/hr), which is into the supersonic regime. Current fighters can easily get themselves down to a speed at which all powers of manoeuvre are lost. The theory to be proven is that if a fighter can continue to manoeuvre under control even below its stalling speed, it will have a tremendous advantage in close combat over a conventional aircraft. If this is confirmed in flight trials by the X-31A, some of the technology may find its way into future fighters, if not the F-22A itself.

In April 1990 the long rumoured 'F-19' was revealed to the world as the Lockheed F-117A, the prototype having first flown nearly nine years earlier. The F-117 designator appears to have arisen from the use of a 117 callsign in the early years, while the F is totally misleading, the aircraft being optimised for attack and defence suppression. A second generation stealth aircraft, its angular shape is comprised of intersecting flat surfaces designed to deflect radar impulses away from any receiver. 37 TFW is the sole operator with 57 aircraft, and is due to redeploy from Tonopah to Holloman during 1992.

Although now supplemented in the interdiction/strike role by the F-15E, the F-111 remains the primary aircraft for this mission, with approximately 370 aircraft of all types including the F-111G, modified from the FB-111A. Tactical ECM is the task of the EF-111A Raven, 42 of which are operated by 42nd and 390th Electronic Combat Squadrons.

The A-10A Warthog has always suffered from the fact that many people could not understand the concept of a slow mover in the close air support/battlefield air interdiction role. Even before the Gulf War it was decided to phase it out in favour of a faster aircraft such as an attack-optimised F-16, and despite the Warthog having performed well against Iraqi ground forces, that decision has not been reversed. A handful of A-10As have been modified for the Forward Air Control (FAC) mission as OA-10As, where their exceptional survivability is a distinct asset. Equiping a number of AFRes and ANG units, the Warthog will be around for a few years yet. Other FAC aircraft, about 60 OA-37B Dragonflies and 75 OV-10A Broncos, remain in service.

Other Commands

No less than five air forces are based within the continental USA. These, with their headquarters are; 1st AF at Langley, Virginia; 8th AF at Barksdale, Louisiana; 9th AF at Shaw, South Carolina; 12th AF at Bergestrom, Texas; and 15th AF at March, California. The ANG HQ is at Andrews in Maryland, while AFRes operates from Robbins in Georgia.

The most important of the overseas commands is USAF Europe (USAFE) with headquarters at Ramstein in Germany. This organisation is dedicated to NATO. In 1991 USAFE consisted of three air forces. These, with their headquarters were; 1st AF at Mildenhall in England; 16th AF at Torrejon in Spain; and 17th AF at Sembach in Germany. With the dissolution of the Warsaw Pact

Below: An A-10 over Turkey just after the Gulf War. The large, slow A-10 performed better in the CAS role than its critics had predicted.

Above: Groundcrew often have to perform their tasks in difficult or uncomfortable conditions, such as in chemical warfare protection suits.

and consequent diminution of the threat, USAFE is undergoing a gradual shrinking process. Many units based in Europe for years have already returned to the USA, while others are to follow in the near future. 16th AF in particular seems to have little future, with the Torrejon-based F-16s leaving Spain.

Pacific Air Forces (PACAF) has its HQ at Hickam in Hawaii, and comprises four air forces. These are 5th AF at Yokota in Japan; 7th AF at Osan in South Korea; 11th AF, formerly Alaskan Air Command, at Elmendorf; and 13th AF, formerly at Clark in the Philippines (closed by a volcanic eruption in 1991), and now at the US Navy base at Subic Bay.

The US Navy

US Naval air power is built around carrier aviation. The giant carriers of the US Navy carry an air wing of up to 90 machines each; both fixed and rotary wing. In fact, a good rule of thumb is one aircraft for each 10,000 tons displacement. The carrier air wing is an autonomous unit, in effect a miniature air force, able to carry out all tasks from air defence through reconnaissance and strike to anti-submarine warfare (ASW).

A typical carrier air wing consists of two squadrons (24 aircraft in total) of F-14 Tomcats for air defence and air superiority; two squadrons (24 aircraft) of F/A-18 Hornet multi-role fighters

Below: Probably the only true multi-role single seat fighter, the F/A-18 Hornet has proven itself over Libya and the Gulf.

Above: On the crowded deck of this carrier can be seen F-14 Tomcats, A-6 Intruders, S-3 Vikings and E-2 Hawkeyes.

for attack, escort, and additional air defence duties; one squadron of ten A-6E Intruders and four KA-6D tankers; four or five EA-6B Prowler EW aircraft; four or five E-2C Hawkeye AEW aircraft; and an ASW complement of ten S-3A Vikings and about six helicopters. Reconnaissance is provided by three standard F-14s fitted with the TARPS system, pending service entry of the dedicated RF-18 Hornet.

At present the USN maintains 14 deployable carrier battle groups, supported by 13 active and two reserve air wings. The Phantom, for so long the mainstay of the fleet, no longer goes to sea, while A-7E Corsair IIs are rapidly being replaced by

Hornets. The legendary A-4 Skyhawk is now only used in the adversary role, for which the USN also operates a handful of remaining F-5Es and 26 F-16Ns.

On 24 December 1991, the F-14 Tomcat reached its 21st birthday. A very agile aircraft, with an unparalleled long range detection and multiple kill capability, the F-14A was badly let down by its engine; the Pratt & Whitney TF30, which was intended only as an interim measure. Finally, it was built with the more powerful and far more reliable GE F110 in 1988, to produce the F-14B. This was to have been followed by the F-14D, with improved radar and avionics, but economics got in the way, and

Above: This F-14 is armed with AIM-7 Sparrows and AIM-9L Sidewinders, photographed during deployment to the Gulf in 1991.

Above: After cancellation of the A-12, the veteran A-6 Intruder will be the main US Navy strike aircraft for the foreseeable future.

only 37 new F-14Ds were authorised, while an upgrade of A and B models to D standard stalled after six aircraft, against a requirement for over 400.

This was very disappointing. The USN has a requirement for an F-14 replacement; this is supposed to be a variant of the Lockheed F-22, suitably navalised and with swing wings to make it carrier compatible. Whether this will happen is uncertain. It seems unlikely, and Grumman have offered an upgraded Tomcat 21 as a cheaper alternative.

First flown in November 1978, the F/A-18 Hornet is a true multi-role aircraft, capable of switching from fighter to attack by at-taching two sensor pods to the fuselage Sparrow positions; a factor which has greatly increased the effectiveness of the carrier air wings. All USN Phantom and most Corsair squadrons have been re-equipped with the type. Hornet C/D is currently the main production model, with upgrades aimed at improving night capability, and a new radar unit is scheduled to enter service in 1994.

The all-weather strike and interdictor aircraft is the A-6E Intruder, which first flew in April 1960. The advanced A-6F, with more powerful and economical engines and a glass cockpit was cancelled in 1989, so this ancient warrior is once more being upgraded, as well as being the subject of rewinging programme. The A-6E was due to be replaced in the middle to late '90s by the A-12 Avenger II, but this was cancelled in early 1991 after cost disputes. McDonnell Douglas have proposed the F/A-18E/F as an interim replacement. This is virtually a scaled up, re-engined, and more capable Hornet, the first flight of which is scheduled for 1995; with IOC planned for 1999.

The US Marine Corps

The task of Marine aviation is to support the ground forces, although USMC squadrons often deploy to sea aboard carriers alongside USN units. Basically there are three Marine Air Wings (MAW), each of which supports a Marine Expeditionary Force (MEF); plus the Marine Reserve. These are 1st MAW at Okinawa supporting 3rd MEF; 2nd MAW at Cherry Point on the east coast of the USA, supporting 2nd MEF; and 3rd MAW at El Toro in California supporting 1st MEF. 4th MEF is the reserve unit with headquarters at New Orleans, with responsibility for supporting Marine reserve forces. In addition there are two Marine Expeditionary Units (MEU) constantly deployed aboard large amphibious vessels, one in the Mediterranean and the other in the western Pacific. MEUs are essentially geared for special operations, and their air component typically consists of half a dozen utility and transport helicopters, four to six AH-1W

Above: An early production F/A-18 Hornet on final acceptance test. This multi-role aircraft entered service in 1984.

Left: An AV-8B sits on the elevator of a US amphibious assault ship. VSTOL aircraft allow such vessels to act as mini-carriers.

SeaCobra attack helicopters, and six AV-8B Harrier IIs.

Like the Navy, the Marine Corps has been going through a re-equipment programme. Hornets finished replacing F-4S Phantoms in regular squadrons during 1989, and the re-equipment of reserve units is nearly completed. A mere handful of F-4S Phantoms now remain with Marine Reserve squadrons.

The specially configured two seater Night Attack F/A-18D, with the rear cockpit dedicated to weapons systems operation, commenced replacing the A-6E in Marine night and all-weather attack squadrons in 1990, and all six F/A-18D squadrons are scheduled to be operational by 1995. This variant of the F/A-18D is only used by the USMC.

The number of A-4 Skyhawks in USMC service is dwindling as these are replaced by AV-8B Harrier IIs. The first Night Attack Harrier was delivered in September 1989, and the next version to enter service is the Harrier II Plus.

Previous USMC Harriers had no real air-to-air capability, but the II Plus will be fitted with the Hughes APG-65 multi-mode radar to rectify this deficiency. In the rotary wing field, the AH-1T SeaCobra has now been virtually replaced by the newer AH-1W SuperCobra.

The USMC Reserve is also being transformed, and by the mid '90s will consist of five F/A-18 and two AV-8B squadrons, while the two AH-1J squadrons will have converted to the AH-1W.

Army Aviation

The US Army and its associated National Guard units are the world's largest operators of rotary wing aircraft, with more than 8,000 machines currently in service. Of these, the attack and anti-tank complement accounts for about 1,600, of which over half are AH-1 Cobras, mainly S or F sub-types armed with TOW missiles.

The spearhead of the anti-tank force is the AH-64A Apache, the total requirement for which is

23

Above: An Army AH-1S Cobra fires a TOW ATGW from the hover. TOW allows helicopters to destroy tanks at extremely long ranges.

807; the majority of which was delivered by January 1992. Prior to the Gulf War, the Apache was criticised for low serviceability rates, but under the pressure of active service and combat conditions, these soared, even in the exacting climatic conditions of the desert. A multi-stage improvement programme was put in hand in 1988, and since then, advanced target acquisition systems have been put in hand, centred on the Longbow millimetric wave radar mounted on a mast through the rotor shaft. The latest plan, announced on 14 October 1991, is in three stages. The first is to upgrade 254 AH-64As to B configuration, with enhanced reliability, communications and navigation kit. The second is to convert 308 AH-64As to C configuration, with the more powerful -701C engines, provision for the Longbow radar and MANPRINT crew stations, with delivery starting in 1995. Finally, 227 AH-64As are to be converted to AH-64Ds, all as the C model but with full Longbow fire control equipment. Delivery of the AH-64D is scheduled for 1996. C and D Apaches will have sufficient commonality to allow them to operate in mixed units.

Much recent thinking has centred on air combat between helicopters. The Apache has the

Below: The AH-64 Apache is fitted with 'Black Hole' IR suppressors to shield the engine exhausts from hand-held heat-seeking SAMs.

speed and agility to be competitive in this field, and recent combat trials have been carried out with both Stinger and Sidewinder missiles in an attempt to give Apache a credible air-to-air weapon.

The US Army has a significant number of light helicopters in the scout/observation/FAC roles, of which the OH-58A/C is the most numerous. This is an elderly design vulnerable to small arms fire, and lacks performance and offensive capability. A successor was sought in the Light Helicopter (LHX) competition which was initiated in 1980. The winner was announced in April 1991 as the Boeing/Sikorsky RAH-66 Comanche. The original requirement was for 2,096 aircraft, but this has now been reduced to 1,292. Comanche is to replace the OH-6, OH-58, and finally the AH-1 and will also operate with and complement the Apache. IOC is scheduled for December 1998.

Combat Colours
Current thinking dictates that concealment is the primary aim of a paint job, although protection against the elements is a fur-

ther consideration. Another is the ever increasing use of radar absorbent materials to lower the radar reflectivity. Shiny aluminum aeroplanes have long disappeared from the combat scene. While the weight of paint on a large aircraft is quite considerable, it is insignificant when set against maximum take-off weight, and there is no point in having an aircraft which is visible from far beyond normal range simply because the sun sparkles on it. Canopy glint can cause the same problem.

The trend towards concealment has been taken to extremes, with low-visibility national markings and small unit insignia, when these exist at all; all conspiring to build up a cloak of anonymity. In beyond visual range (BVR) combat, however, when shooting at opponents seen only on radar, it would not effect the combat one iota if they were painted purple! But in most cases combats will close down to visual distance very quickly, where paint jobs take on increasing importance in providing concealment. Deception camouflage, intended to disguise the aspect of the aircraft, and

Below: Many US tactical aircraft have adopted two shades of grey for camouflage purposes, such as this F-16.

Above: Used by the Army as a light observation helicopter, the OH-58D Kiowa has a stabilised sensor mast above the main rotor.

therefore what it is doing next, has also been tried. One of the more interesting experiments was painting a dummy canopy in black on the underside. This was not adopted by the US, as the consensus of opinon is that if you are close enough to see it, you are too close to be fooled by it. Nevertheless, Canadian Hornets use this device.

There are two schools of thought here. The official line is that the greatest degree of invisibility should be sought, as the side that sees first gains the initiative. Dissenting voices point out that the probability of mistaken identity, and possible 'blue on blue' engagements, rises sharply, as does the risk of midair collisions, not only in war, but in peacetime training. Vietnam ace Randall Cunningham is on record as saying, after the epic multi-bogey close combat on 10 May 1972, that some form of large and easily identifiable 'buzz number' would have helped considerably in identifying friendly aircraft with whom he wished to co-ordinate attack or defence manoeuvres. Also, in the October War of 1973 in the Middle East, the Israelis painted large black edged orange triangles on the wings of their Mirages to assist in identification, even at the risk of making them more visible.

For many years the standard paint job consisted of dark on top and light undersides, the idea being to hide from predators above by merging with the ground, while being less visible against the sky to ground defences. Like countershading, which contrasted dark colours with highlights, this presupposed that tactical aircraft only fly wings level at high noon. An aircraft rolling inverted to pull down immediately flashed a pale underside, in what became known in USAF circles as the 'Ivan thanks you very much' manoeuvre.

Two basic forms of camouflage were finally adopted by the USAF. For medium and high altitude missions, such as air superiority or EW, one or more shades of light/medium grey are used to enable the aircraft to blend in with a sky or cloud background. For low level interdiction, attack and close air support, a more traditional green/grey, or green/grey/brown irregular pattern is used, carried right across the underside. To a

Above: Hardened aircraft shelters allow maintenance and re-arming to take place in conditions of security and comfort.

ground observer, the colour of the underside of an aircraft hardly matters, as when contrasted against sky or clouds it always looks dark.

Operational theatres also affect paint jobs. When the A-10A was first deployed to Europe, experiments were carried out to determine which scheme would give the most effective conceal-ment against a fighter flying higher. They included some startling lozenge patterns, which rejoiced in the unofficial names of 'Measles' and 'Afrika Corps Revisited' among others. The final choice was a European 1; a conventional irregular pattern of two greens and a grey. One odd-ball in the camouflage field is of course the F-117A, which is all

Below: The Marine Corps use a three-tone blue/grey colour scheme on their AH-1W SeaCobra attack helicopters.

over matt black for night operations.

The USN, which flies most of its operations over the sea, opts for low-vis grey finishes for both air superiority and attack aircraft, as this is considered the best compromise. The Marine Corps uses two tone air superiority grey on its Hornets, but dark green/grey camouflage on its AV-8Bs and SeaCobras. Army attack helicopters are generally finished in olive drab, although this can be altered to suit local conditions.

Even before the Gulf War, saner counsels were beginning to prevail. In the USAF, black tail codes, occasionally with white highlighting, were coming back into use, together with coloured fin stripes of the 'hippy headband' type, making individual aircraft rather more easily identifiable in a close combat situation. But with the deployment of A-10As from Europe to the Gulf, it was immediately noticeable that unit markings vanished, although this was not the case with home-based 'hogs. Desert paint schemes were experimented with in the USA, including a two-tone pink, but in the Kuwait Theatre of Operations (KTO), all A-10As retained their European 1 colours, albeit rather faded.

The B-52Gs operating from Fairford were notable for having their fin insignia deleted, although nose art was carried on some birds. This was however not the case with some other USAF units. The F-15Es of 4th TFW were just one example of a unit which continued to carry fin stripes, and highlighted black/white tail codes and numbers.

The USN stayed mainly with low-vis markings, although these included large unit insignia on the fins. But even before the Gulf crisis, a move had been made to return to old style unit markings. One notable example was CVW-14, aboard USS *Independence*, some of whose aircraft sported brightly coloured tails reminiscent of the pre-Vietnam era. High-vis squadron insignia were also seen on the tails of some CVW-1 (USS *America*) aircraft. In the Gulf, Marine and Army machines, generally, but not always, adopted desert camouflage, while helicopters operating in the battle zone once the land war had started, carried

Below: This F-16 flying over northern Iraq immediately after the Gulf War shows how some 'high-vis' markings have come back into use.

'D-Day' style black/white invasion stripes on their tail booms as an aid to identification for ground troops.

One of the features of the Gulf War was the proliferation of nose art. SAC had always encouraged this, both as a morale booster and a maintainer of tradition, but on arrival in Saudi Arabia, much of it was ordered to be removed, as it was felt that scantily clad 'ladies' would offend the sensibilities of the host nation. Be this as it may, nose art proliferated in the theatre, covering the gamut from the aforementioned ladies through cartoon characters to more warlike and heraldic emblems. Kill and mission markings were also widespread. Most nose art was removed once the units returned to their home bases, but some, especially kill markings, remains in situ.

Below: The Gulf War will probably be the last operational action of the A-7 Corsair light attack aircraft in US service.

Bell AH-1 HueyCobra/
SeaCobra/SuperCobra

AH-1J, S, T, F, W

Origin: Bell Helicopter Textron, Fort Worth.
Type: Close-support and attack helicopter.
Engine: (AH-1J) One 1,800shp P&W Canada T400 Twin Pac rated at
1,100shp; (S) 1,800shp T53-703; (T) 2,050shp T400-WV-402; (F) one
1,800shp T53-L-703; (W) two 1,690shp T700-GE-401.
Dimensions: Diameter of two-blade main rotor (J,S,F) 44ft (13.41m); (T, W)
48ft (14.63m); overall length rotors turning (J, S) 53ft 4in (16.26m); (F) 53ft
1in (16.18m); (T,W) 58ft (17.68m); height (all) 13ft 6in (4.11m).
Weights: Empty (J) 7,261lb (3,294kg); (S) 6,479lb (2,939kg); (T) 8,608lb
(3,904kg); (F) 6,598lb (2,993kg); (W) 10,200lb (4,627kg); Max: (J,S,F) 10,000lb
(4,535kg); (T) 14,000lb (6,350kg); (W) 14,750lb (6,690kg).
Performance: Max speed (J) 180kt (333km/hr); (S, T, F) with TOW 123kt
(227km/hr); (W) 152kt (282km/hr); initial climb rate (J) 1,090ft/min
(5.53m/sec); (S, F, T, W) 1,620ft/min (8.23m/sec); range (J, S, T) 310nm
(574km); (F) 274nm (507km); (W) 343nm (635km).
Armament: (F,W) one M197 three barrel 20mm cannon with 750 rounds in
nose turret; eight BGM-81 TOW anti-tank missiles or four 2.75in (70mm)
rocket pods; (W only) eight AGM-114 Hellfire anti-tank missiles in lieu of
TOW; two AIM-9L Sidewinder air-to-air or two AGM-122A Sidearm anti-
radiation missiles; grenade dispensers or Minigun pods.
History: First flight 1965, (T) 20 May 1976, (F) 1979; (W) April 1980.
Users: US Army, USMC.

Development: Considered to be a revolutionary design when it first appeared
in the late 1960s, the AH-1 HueyCobra was developed by Bell as a private venture
and established the standard of layout for a generation of anti-tank helicopters.
Using the basic rotor, engine and transmission system of the UH-1 utility transport,
the AH-1 incorporated a streamlined, thin-profile fuselage with a gunner seated
in the nose in front of the raised pilot position and an armament consisting of
a chin-mounted gun supplemented by weapons pylons under the stub wings.
This basic arrangement has been followed by similar designs currently being
developed in Italy (Agusta A129), Germany (PAH-2 proposals) and even the Soviet
Union (Mil Mi-28 Havoc, although this is more akin to the AH-64 Apache).

The AH-1G was the first production version of the Cobra for the US Army;
1,116 were built, the type accumulating more than one million flight hours in
South-East Asia. In 1972 the first missile-armed Cobra, the AH-1Q fitted with
the tube-launched TOW, was tested. A total of 92 were built, but performance
was somewhat limited when the helicopter operated with a full load of eight
rounds. This problem was resolved by increasing the engine power and uprating
the transmission to produce the AH-1S, and all the Qs and 200 Gs were converted

Above: Flat plate transparencies, seen here on this AH-1F, are a low observables measure intended to reduce sun reflection scatter.

Left: 'Canned Heat' was an early HueyCobra which saw extensive service in Vietnam.

Below: The AH-1Q was the first Cobra to be armed with guided missiles, in this case the tube-launched wire guided AGM-71 TOW.

to S standard beginning in 1977. In addition to the conversions, 100 new AH-1Ss were produced to meet an Army shortfall in anti-tank helicopters, followed by a further batch of 98 which were known as Step 2 machines.

The Modernised AH-1S or Step 3 variant has more enhancements to improve the type's battlefield performance, not least in its capacity to operate throughout its full flight spectrum with eight TOWs. Its equipment fit includes a laser rangefinder, a Doppler navigation set, an engine heat suppressor to reduce IR signature, an IR jammer, and RWR linked with an AN/ALQ-136 jamming system. A low-glint, flat glass canopy replaces the original rounded type, and the rotor blades are made of lightweight composite materials.

The most recent, and probably the final variant of the HueyCobra for the US Army is the AH-1F. This apparently retrograde suffix arose from a plethora of AH-1S modifications, and to avoid confusion, three suffixes which had previously been used on earlier UH-1 models, all of which were by now out of service, had been revived for the AH series. The AH-1F was originally the AH-1S(MOD), and the F designator was not adopted until 1987.

The prototypes for the AH-1F were two AH-1Ps, which suitably modified, began trials with the Army in July 1979. The main changes are a new fire control system, including a laser rangefinder, a laser tracker set, a digital ballistics computer for gunnery solutions, and a Kaiser HUD. Survivability is enhanced by an AN/APR-39 RWR; AN/ALQ-144 IR jamming equipment, and a 'black hole' IR exhaust suppressor. Delivery of the AH-1F began in November 1979, with the first of 149 new-build aircraft while 378 AH-1Gs were also upgraded to this more powerful standard.

In the mid-1960s the US Marine Corps also saw a requirement for an attack helicopter and ordered 38 AH-1Gs, the first of which was delivered in February 1969; a further 67 twin-engined AH-1J SeaCobras followed, and by 1982 the Corps had received 51 improved AH-1Ts, some equipped with TOW.

The ultimate development in the Cobra series is the AH-1W SuperCobra, previously known as the AH-1T+. With two General Electric T700-401 turboshafts, the 1W is far more powerful than its predecessors, has better performance, and carries a much wider range of armament. The TOW anti-tank missiles can be substituted by long-ranged laser-guided Hellfires; while to provide

Below: The AH-1W SuperCobra is used by the US Marine Corps. This example carries AGM-114A Hellfire missiles in lieu of TOW.

an air-to-air capability against other helicopters or even fixed wing aircraft, it can mount a pair of Sidewinders or Stingers. Sidearm anti-radiation missiles for the defence suppression role can also be mounted.

The SuperCobra is operated by the US Marines only, as the Army has elected to wait for the RAH-66 Comanche to team with its very capable Apache fleet. The first new-build machine entered service on 27 March 1986 and production still continues, while many AH-1Ts are to be converted.

Many HueyCobras, SeaCobras and SuperCobras took part in the Gulf War, where they gave sterling service, even though in part overshadowed by the formidable Apache.

Above: Marine Corps AH-1Ws often undergo training in desert conditions — a policy which paid off in the 1991 Gulf War.

Boeing B-52 Stratofortress

B-52G, H

Origin: Boeing Airplane Company (from May 1961 The Boeing Company), Seattle, Washington.

Type: Heavy bomber and missile platform.

Engines: (B-52G) Eight 13,750lb (6,237kg) thrust P&WA J57-43W or -43WB turbojets, (H) eight 17,000lb (7,711kg) thrust P&WA TF33-1 or -3 turbofans.

Dimensions: Span 185ft (56.39m); length (G/H) as built) 157ft 7in (48m), (G/H modified) 160ft 11in (49.05m); height (G/H) 40ft 8in (12.4m); wing area 4,000 sq ft (371.6m²).

Weights: Empty about 195,000lb (88,450kg); Max take-off 488,000lb (221,355kg); this can only be exceeded in flight (i.e. after in-flight refuelling), under Emergency War Order conditions.

Performance: Max speed (clean) 516kt (957km/hr); penetration speed at low altitude about 352kt (652km/hr, Mach 0.53); service ceiling (G) 46,000ft (14,020m), (H) 47,000ft (14,325m); range on max fuel with no external ordnance, optimum high altitude cruise (G) 7,300nm (13,528km), (H) 8,800nm (16,307km); take-off run (G) 10,000ft (3,048m), (H) 9,500ft (2,895m).

Armament: (G) four 0.5in (12.7mm) heavy machine guns in remotely operated tail turret with ASG-15 fire control system, up to 12 AGM-86B cruise missiles and eight SRAM II air-to-surface missiles; eight freefall nuclear or 51 iron bombs, Popeye and Harpoon ASMs. (H) as G but with one six barrel 20mm cannon in tail turret.

History: First flight 15 April 1952.

User: Air Combat Command (USAF).

Development: Modifications and expensive upgrade programmes have kept the 30-year-old B-52 Stratofortress design in line with modern weapon delivery and attack techniques so that this impressive aircraft continues to be a valuable asset. Two variants remain in USAF service: the B-52G, of which 192 were built

Above: Beneath the nose of this B-52G are the bulges of the EVS (Electro-optical Viewing System), just one of the many modifications which have given the legendary Boeing giant the ability to continue in service long after its quarter-century.

Left: B-52G 57-6518 loaded with AGM-69A SRAM missiles on underwing hardpoints. For years these huge aircraft stood ready for 24 hours a day as part of the nuclear deterrent triad, but with the ending of the Cold War, the nuclear adapted B-52Gs are being phased out, along with the FB-111 strategic bombers.

Right: A B-52G Stratofortress makes its characteristic flat approach for landing. Boeing engineers helped to make the pilot's job easier at this stage of flight by building in large 'barn door' flaps and spoilers to slow the aircraft down to an acceptable speed. The large plant at Wichita delivered 193 B-52G models between 1958 and 1961 before production switched to the B-52H. Identification features of the G compared with the F include a shorter fin, spoilers in place of ailerons for lateral control, a shortened nose radome and a remote tail gun.

Above: This B-52G was used as a trials aircraft for advanced ECM equipment and is seen here contrailing dramatically at high altitude.

Right: Recognisable by the TF33 turbofan engines and their enlarged front cowls, this B-52H also has the low-level equipment fit and the 700-gallon underwing fuel tanks shown on the G version above.

with deliveries beginning in February 1959; and the B-52H, the final version, which has TF33 turbofans (giving an increased range of more than 10,000 miles) and improved defensive armament including a 20mm Vulcan multi-barrel gun and of which 102 were delivered from May 1961. Of these, 166 B-52Gs and 95 B-52Hs remain in service as at 1992.

As the penetration part of the mission was to be flown at low level, the big B-52s were given an Electro-optical Viewing System (EVS), situated in blisters around the nose, using forward looking infra-red and low light TV sensors, allied to terrain avoidance equipment, to improve the aircraft's chances of getting to its target in any weather, day or night. Avionics improvements include ALQ-122 Smart Noise Operation Equipment and AN/ALQ-155(V) electronic countermeasures kit, satellite communications equipment, tail warning radar and ALQ-172 jammers. All are designed to help the aircraft survive against sophisticated enemy defences.

With the service entry of the B-1B Lancer as the main USAF manned penetrator, the B-52 became a stand-off missile carrier, and was modified accordingly. Its main weapon is the AGM-86B Air Launched Cruise Missile (ALCM), twelve of which are carried on underwing pylons, plus eight SRAM IIs or other weapons internally on a Common (to the B-1B as well) Strategic Rotary Launcher (CSRL). In all, 98 B-52Gs and 95 B-52Hs were modified for the nuclear delivery role in this way, while the rest were equipped for the conventional bombing mission. Five of the twelve B-52 Bomb Wings were assigned to this task as at 1992,

Left: Camouflaged for the current low-level penetration role, this B-52G is fitted with FLIR/LLTV 'bumps' around the nose.

Above: B-52s were extensively used in the Gulf War of 1991, flying from bases in the continental USA, UK, Spain, and the Indian Ocean.

Above: More than 25,700 tons of ordnance, 41 percent of the total dropped by the USAF during the Gulf War was delivered by B-52s.

while a retirement programme to phase out the nuclear-mission adapted B-52Gs had begun earlier.

Another mission for which some B-52Gs have been converted is long range maritime support. For this, thirty aircraft have been fitted out to carry eight AGM-84 Harpoon anti-ship missiles externally. There are two squadrons, one based at Loring AFB, Maine, to support operations in the Atlantic; the other based at Anderson AFB on Guam, supporting operations in the Pacific rim area. All B-52Gs fitted out for conventional warfare have an integrated conventional stores management system, which enables them to carry a wide variety of smart or dumb weapons, including the Israeli-designed Popeye AGM (*Have Nap*), by means of removable software cassettes to change the programming as required.

With the reduction of the Soviet threat in the late '80s and the consequent stand-down of Strategic Air Command, the role of the B-52 as a nuclear deterrent seems to be over. The type performed admirably in South East Asia where, after area bombing the countryside where Viet Cong forces were supposed to be, its career climaxed with the conventional bombing of Hanoi in December 1972. Then in early 1991 it once again demonstrated its global reach, bombing targets in Iraq. B-52s flew 1,624 missions in the Gulf War, dropping some 72,000 weapons totalling more than 25,700 tons, while operating from bases in England, Spain, and the Indian Ocean. This amounted to 41 per cent of all USAF ordnance dropped during the conflict. A considerable amount of this tonnage was aimed at dug-in Republican Guard units. Details of the material damage caused by these raids are not forthcoming and area bombing of such diffuse targets is not terribly effective measured by these standards. On the other hand, the morale effect of cells of giant B-52s raining down bombs by the hundred must have been devastating, and it is in this difficult to assess field that the contribution of the B-52 force to the liberation of Kuwait must be judged. The one true measure that we have is the incredibly light casualty list of the allied ground forces, against which, B-52 operations must be judged to be successful.

Below: Its eight engines belching smoke at full throttle, a heavily laden B-52 takes off en-route for targets in Iraq and Kuwait.

Boeing Sikorsky RAH-66 Comanche

RAH-66A

Origin: Boeing Helicopters Division of Philadelphia and United Technologies Sikorsky Aircraft Division of Stratford, Connecticut.
Type: Reconnaissance/attack helicopter.
Engines: Two 925shp (690kW) LHTEC (Allison and Garrett) T800-LHT-800 turboshafts with transmission rated at 2,054shp (1,532kW).
Dimensions: Diameter of five bladed rotor 39ft 0½in (11.90m); overall length (rotors turning) 46ft 10in (14.28m); length of fuselage/fin 43ft 3½in (13.22m); height 11ft 1½in (3.39m).
Weights: Empty 7,500lb (3,402kg); primary mission 10,112lb (4,587kg); self deploy 17,714lb (7,790kg).
Performance: Max speed 177kt (328km/hr); with external stores 165kt (306km/hr); vertical rate of climb 1,182ft/min (6m/sec); self deploy range 1,260nm (2,335km).
Armament: One 20mm twin-barrelled cannon in turret under the nose with 500 rounds, rate of fire 1,500 rounds/min; reconnaissance mission, four AGM-114 Hellfire and two AIM-92 Stinger; maximum weapons load (internal and external) 14 Hellfire or 18 Stinger.
History: Programme start 1980, team formed June 1985, contract award 5 April 1991, first flight scheduled September 1994, IOC scheduled December 1998.
User: US Army.

Development: One of the strangest aircraft development programmes of recent times has been the Light Helicopter Experimental (LHX) for the US Army. Initiated in 1980, LHX was intended to replace something like 8,000 existing machines with two basic models, LHX SCAT (SCout ATtack) and LHX Utility. Bedevilled by lack of funding, this tremendously ambitious programme called for advanced capabilities, including a high degree of one-man operation. As the decade crept on, the goalposts were moved from time to time, and requirements like air combat and low observables came increasingly to figure on the shopping lists.

In the early stages there was the Advanced Rotorcraft Technology Integration (ARTI) programme. Basically an examination of possibilities, this dragged on for some considerable time. In 1985, the sheer size of the potential programme caused contenders to team up, a process rendered risible by Boeing/Sikorsky calling themselves 'The First Team', only to be capped by Bell/McDonnell Douglas adopting the title of 'The SuperTeam'.

Funding constraints ruled out the possibility of prototypes being built to take part in a flyoff. A development contract award for hardware would be made on the basis of the evaluation of Mission Equipment Packages (MEPs), and a demonstration and validation programme began in earnest in October 1988, lasting for 23 months. Naturally a great deal of emphasis was placed on breadboard demonstrations and simulations. The decision was announced on 5 April 1991; the Boeing/Sikorsky team were awarded a contract for the further development of what had now become the RAH-66A Comanche. This is to involve the first flying hardware; four prototype Comanches to be built during the demonstration/validation phase, with first flight scheduled for September

Below: The RAH-66 Comanche, seen here in mock-up form, shows the first steps towards producing a stealthy helicopter, perhaps the most remarkable feature of which is the smoothly shaped rotor head.

1994. A further two will be built during the engineering and manufacturing development phase which follows.

By this time, the utility variant had long fallen by the wayside and the programme size had shrunk considerably, firstly to 2,096, then to 1,292 machines.

The Comanche as proposed is a very interesting machine. Almost entirely of composite construction, it has a five bladed bearingless main rotor. This gives a low blade loading, which not only reduces acoustic signature but provides a significant reduction in vibration levels. The tail rotor is enclosed in what the French would call a fenestron, but Boeing/Sikorsky call the FANTAIL anti-torque system, on top of which is a high set T tail. Landing gear is fully retractable.

The flight control system is digital electronic, while the crew stations are optimised for low work load with CRT screens and wide field-of-view helmet mounted displays. Night and adverse weather operation will be aided by a second generation focal plane (staring) array FLIR, and image intensifiers. The FLIR is also part of the targeting system, which includes Low Light Level TV (LLTV), a laser rangefinder/designator and a target detection/classification system.

Although helicopters by their very nature do not readily lend themselves to low observables technology, certain stealth measures have been incorporated, among them the now almost obligatory flat panel cockpit transparencies, combined with a certain amount of faceting, although not to the same degree as used by the F-117A. It is however interesting to note that the losing Bell/McDonnell Douglas LHX contender featured smoothly rounded transparencies, a highly streamlined fuselage, and the rotorless NOTAR anti-torque system.

One of the greatest dangers to battlefield helicopters comes from shoulder-launched IR homing missiles. Boeing/Sikorsky claim to have eliminated the IR emissions on which these normally home. The two turboshafts exhaust through cones into the tailboom, together with heated air from the avionics bay which is situated behind the weapons bay. Cold air is then drawn in through grilles behind the main rotor shaft to mix with and cool the heated exhaust gases before being expelled along flat downward facing panels on both sides of the tail boom. This is stated to make it virtually impossible for a heat-seeking missile to lock on to the helicopter.

Radar signature reduction measures are mainly classified, although the use of faceting to deflect impulses away from the emitter is one very visible method, and the extensive use of radar absorbent materials (RAM) can be assumed.

Below: Maximum load of 14 AGM-114 Hellfires, three on each open weapons bay door, and eight on demountable stub-wings.

Above: With no external pylons and the weapons bay doors closed, this example is configured for the stealthy reconnaissance mission.

External carriage of weapons has been largely avoided, as these make great radar reflectors. Up to six Hellfires can be mounted internally on the weapons bay doors, which can be opened in a matter of seconds. These doors also double as engine maintenance platforms. On missions where stealth is less important, external stores carriage systems can be fitted and loaded within 20 minutes, giving a further eight Hellfires or a Stinger/Hellfire combination.

Light weight and high capability requirements inevitably end in a tradeoff, and so it has proved with Comanche. In early 1992, production weight estimates showed a 300lb (136kg) increase over the projected basic, while an extra 963lb (437kg) has been added by the US Army as a result of Gulf War experience. This includes more crew armour, HF radio, and IR and ECM equipment. In addition, all RAH-66s are to be capable of carrying the Longbow mast-mounted fire control radar, although only one third will be so equipped, which calls for a further 540lb (245kg) capability. Extra power is needed to cope with the added weight, and LHTEC has been asked to uprate the T800 turboshafts by 12 per cent.

The US Army is scheduled to receive 1,292 Comanches, with deliveries starting in 1997 for IOC the following year.

Below: Due to make its first flight in September 1994, Comanche is a light reconnaissance/attack machine intended to supplement Apache.

Cessna A-37 Dragonfly

A-37B, OA-37B

Origin: Cessna Aircraft Company, Wichita, Kansas.
Type: Light attack/forward air control aircraft.
Engines: Two 2,850lb (1,293kg) thrust GE J85-17A turbojets.
Dimensions: Span (over tanks) 35ft 10½in (10.93m); length (exc refuelling probe) 28ft 3¼in (8.62m); wing area 183.9 sq ft (17.09m²).
Weights: Empty 6,211lb (2,817kg); loaded 14,000lb (6,350kg).
Performance: Max speed 440kt (816km/hr); normal cruising speed (clean) 425kt (787km/hr); initial climb rate 6,990ft/min (35.50m/sec); service ceiling 41,765ft (12,730m); range (max fuel, four drop tanks) 879nm (1,628km); (max ordnance load) 400nm (741km).
Armament: GAU-2B/A 7.62mm Minigun in fuselage; eight underwing pylons (four inners 870lb, 394kg, each, next 600lb, 272kg, and outers 500lb, 227kg) for large numbers of weapons, pods, dispensers, clusters, launchers or recon/EW equipment.
History: First flight 22 October 1963.
Users: ACC, PACAF, ANG.

Development: Cessna's diminutive Dragonfly ranks as just about the smallest low-cost combat aircraft in the US Air Force. Its success in the attack role stems from the company's experience in designing pilots' aeroplanes, easy to handle and with good responses and positive control, virtues which were particularly

Above: The A-37B Dragonfly is the only USAF combat aircraft small enough to allow the pilot to stand and look down into the cockpit.

Below: An excellent aircraft for counter-insurgency work, the A-37B is now only used by the USAF for Forward Air Control under the designation OA-37B. Vulnerable in the face of modern counter air weapons, it is being replaced by the much more rugged OA-10A.

evident in the T-37 basic trainer, which was produced in large numbers for the USAF and became the basis for the development of the A-37.

The steady increase in guerrilla actions around the world was one factor that led the USAF to consider a less expensive 'bomb truck' to meet a counter-insurgency requirement at the beginning of the 1960s. After all, it was hardly cost-effective to use one of the Century-series fighters to haul iron bombs across a few miles of territory to hit (or more likely miss) two or three dissidents in the jungle! So the YAT-37D evolved. The wings were strengthened and eventually accommodated eight underwing hardpoints, and a GAU-2 7.62mm Minigun with 1,500 rounds of ammunition was installed in the nose. The two crew members were given cockpit armour, the fuel tanks were made self-sealing and the undercarriage was beefed up to take the greater weight.

Vietnam was the proving ground for the 39 A-37As built, and the experience gained was used to help produce the definitive A-37B, 550 of which were assembled before production ended in 1975. A refuelling probe was fitted in the nose, reticulated foam was added to the fuel tanks to protect against fire or explosion if hit by incendiary AA rounds, and the thrust line of the two J85 engines was moved slightly outwards and downwards.

The Dragonfly proved highly successful during the latter stages of the Vietnam War, although even the most experienced pilot found survival difficult when the North Vietnamese brought large numbers of automatic AA weapons into the South. Some South Vietnamese Air Force A-37Bs were captured by the invading forces and were used by the North for some time.

Until the early 'eighties, the main task of the 'Tweet', as the Dragonfly is widely known, has been counter-insurgency (COIN), and in this role, A-37Bs were transferred from the regular Air Force to ANG and AF Reserve squadrons during the post-Vietnam period. Then in the early 'eighties, the type was reassigned to Forward Air Control, with the new designation of OA-37B, in which it replaced the much slower, less capable, and more vulnerable O-2 Skymaster. Small and agile, it was well suited to this mission, although it was disadvantaged in not having ejector seats. In the event of having to abandon ship, the two man crew were forced to dive over the side, and at the low levels at which the FAC mission is generally flown, this was far from satisfactory, especially as it meant avoiding

Left: Two A-37Bs of the Air Force Reserve undergo ground handling between missions. The side-by-side trainer origin of this design is plain, but the tactical camouflage adds a certain warlike appearance to what is one of the more attractive combat jets. With 550 built and only some 60 currently in USAF service, spare A-37s have found their way to a number of Central American and Asian air forces.

Below: A Reserve pilot pre-flights his aircraft. The A-37 lacks ejection seats, so to bail out in an emergency the crew have to step over the side of the cockpit.

the wing leading edge with the engine inlet just beneath it. The OA-37B can be regarded as not much more than a stopgap solution, although it is faster and more agile than the OV-10A Bronco which also flies the FAC mission. In early 1992, it was being phased out in favour of the far more survivable OA-10A Warthog, with only about 60 OA-37Bs remaining in service.

Fairchild A-10 Thunderbolt II

A-10A, OA-10A

Origin: Fairchild Republic Company, Farmingdale, New York.
Type: Close-support attack aircraft.
Engines: Two 9,065lb (4,112kg) thrust GE TF34-100 turbofans.
Dimensions: Span 57ft 6in (17.53m); length 53ft 4in (16.26m); height
14ft 8in (4.47m); wing area 506 sq ft (47m²).
Weights: Empty 21,519lb (9,761kg); forward airstrip weight (no fuel but four
Mk 82 bombs and 750 rounds) 32,730lb (14,846kg); max 50,000lb
(22,680kg); operating weight empty 24,918lb (11,302kg).
Performance: Max speed 390kt (723km/hr); never-exceed dive speed
450kt (834km/hr); initial climb rate 6,000ft/min (30.47m/sec); service ceiling
45,000ft (13,715m); take-off distance 1,200-4,000ft (366-1,219m) dependent
on weight; landing distance 2,000ft (610m); operating radius for CAS
mission with 1.8hr loiter plus reserves, 250nm (461km); radius for deep
strike penetration 540nm (1,000km); ferry range with allowances 2,208nm
(4,092km).
Armament: One GAU-8/A Avenger 30mm seven-barrel gun with 1,174
rounds; total external ordnance load of 16,000lb (7,257kg) hung on eleven
pylons, three side-by-side on body and four under each wing; several
hundred combinations of stores up to individual weight of 5,000lb (2,268kg)
with max total weight 14,638lb (6,640kg) with full internal fuel.
History: First flight (YA-10A) 10 May 1972, (production A-10A) 21 October
1975.
Users: ACC, PACAF, USAFE, ANG, AFRes.

Development: The A-10A Thunderbolt is the US Air Force's principal fixed-wing
anti-armour close air support aircraft. With a cockpit perched on a simple box-
structure fuselage, two big fan engines aft and twin fins and rudders, this strange
design takes no prizes for good looks, but its basic ugliness compared with most
contemporary combat aircraft is the result of careful planning aimed at giving
the A-10 as much chance as possible of surviving over the battlefield.

Fairchild engineers designed the A-10 to meet a USAF requirement stemming
from experience in the Vietnam War and calling for a heavily armoured anti-
tank aircraft capable of carrying a weighty ordnance load over long distances.

**Below: The unique layout of the Warthog is entirely due to its
optimisation for survivability and low speed agility.**

Above: The seven barrel GAU-8/A Avenger, the muzzles of which are seen here, is the most powerful aircraft gun ever flown.

The result was a rugged aircraft with eleven ventral weapons pylons and a tank-killing GAU-8 30mm multi-barrel cannon in the nose capable of disabling most current Soviet AFVs. In cases of ground-fire damage or spares problems, certain parts of the structure, such as the flaps, main undercarriage units and movable tail surfaces, are interchangeable. Both the tail unit and the fuselage act as partial shields for the two engines, masking their infra-red signature and lessening the probability of a hit by a heat-seeking missile.

Survivability is the key to successful A-10 operations, and the aircraft is intended to work with as little external support equipment as possible. Apart from the unique cannon loading system, the A-10 is able to sit on the ground during turn-rounds using one engine or its APU to keep its systems alive. Then, loaded with Maverick ASMs or Rockeye cluster bombs, an A-10 can fly for 30 minutes to the target area and operate for an hour hunting in packs of, say, four aircraft, responding to calls from ground controllers and co-operating with US Army AH-64 Apache helicopters in co-ordinated attacks on enemy armour. Enhancing the aircraft's capability is the Pave Penny laser target designator pod which can be fitted below the cockpit.

Below: The unusual location of the turbofans of the A-10 is designed to take advantage of masking offered by the tail surfaces.

The A-10 has few vices, and is capable of positive control response when manoeuvring at low level. Aircrew fly it from 1,000ft (300m) down to 50ft (15m) in one-mile visibility along valleys, round hills, and among the trees across the flat plains of Central Europe. It is not a fast aircraft: it cannot be if pilots are to acquire a target visually and attack it. In an ideal situation, a tank can be picked up at a range of 6,000ft (1,800m) by an A-10 flying at around 300-350kts, and a burst of 30mm would reach the target in 2.3 seconds. SAMs and radar-directed AA guns are the A-10's biggest enemies, followed by opposing fighters and armed helicopters. In order to provide a credible air defence capability against enemy fighters and helicopters, AIM-9L Sidewinders were carried on twin launchers on the outboard wing hardpoints from the late 'eighties.

The survivability of the slow moving close air support machine was always in question, and in 1989 it was decided to replace the A-10A with a fast jet. Of the 645 Warthogs in the inventory in August 1990, 155 were earmarked for conversion to OA-10As to replace OA-37Bs in the FAC role, with the most of the remainder going into storage when they could be replaced by F-16s.

The Warthog played a minor role in the invasion of Grenada in the late 'eighties, but its real baptism of fire came in the Gulf War in 1991. In all, 144 'hogs' were deployed to the area, and these flew almost 8,100 missions. They destroyed large numbers of Iraqi tanks, guns, and other vehicles, plus a few radar sites and mobile Scud launchers, losing five of their number while doing so. Losses would have been far higher had not the survivability measures performed as advertised. The Gulf War also saw the combat debut of the OA-10A in the FAC role. After the cessation of hostilities, it was wondered in some quarters whether the proven effectiveness of the A-10A would earn it a reprieve. But this was not to be.

Above: A low level pass by a Warthog dropping retarded munitions. In this case the retarding agent is the ballute (balloon/parachute).

Below: Typical warload in the Gulf conflict was two AGM-65 Mavericks, two AIM-9 Sidewinders and one ALQ-119 ECM pod.

General Dynamics F-16 Fighting Falcon

F-16A, B, C, D, N, RF-16.

Origin: General Dynamics Corporation, Fort Worth, Texas.

Type: Multirole single seat fighter with two-seat trainer

Engine: (A, B, C, D) one F100-PW-220 afterburning turbofan rated at 23,770lb (10,782kg); (some Block 40/42 C, D) F110-GE-100 afterburning turbofan rated at 28,982lb (13,146kg); (C, D, Block 50) F110-GE-129 and (C,D, Block 52) F100-PW-229 afterburning turbofan, both in the 29,000lb (13,154kg) thrust class.

Dimensions: Span 31ft (9.45m); over wingtip missiles 32ft 10in (10.01m); length (all, exc. probe) 47ft 7¾in (14.52m); height (all) 16ft 8½in (5.09m); wing area 300 sq ft (27.87m²).

Weights: Empty (A) 16,292lb (7,390kg); (B) 16,904lb (7,668kg); (C-F100) 18,238lb (8,273kg); (C-F110) 19,020lb (8,627kg); (D-F100) 18,726lb (8,494kg); (D-F110) 19,517lb (8,853kg); max take-off (A,B) 37,500lb (17,010kg); (C,D) 42,300lb (19,184kg).

Performance: (Clean with two AIM-9s); max speed at altitude (A) Mach 2.05; (C Block 40) Mach 1.86; (C Block 50) Mach 2. Max speed at sea level; (all) Mach 1.21; initial climb rate (all) exceeding 50,000ft/min (254m/sec); service ceiling (A,C Block 40) 57,000ft (17,373m); (C Block 50/52) 61,000ft (18,592m); tactical radius with four Mk 84 bombs and centreline tank, (A) 430nm (797km); (C Block 40) 360nm (667km); (C Block 50/52) 350nm (649km); Ferry range (all) approx. 2,100nm (3,892km).

Armament: One GE M61A-1 20mm gun with 515 rounds; centreline pylon for 300 US gal (1,136l) drop tank or 2,200lb (998kg) bomb, inboard and middle wing pylons for 3,500lb (1,587kg) each, outer wing pylons for 250lb (113.4kg).

History: First flight (YF-16) 20 January 1974, (production A) 7 August 1978; service delivery (A) 17 August 1978, (C/D) 1984, (C/D Block 40/42) 1989, (C/D Block 50/52) 1992.

Users: ACC, PACAF, USAFE, ANG, AFRes, USN.

Above: Originally designed as an austere air superiority fighter, with two wingtip mounted AIM-9L Sidewinders and a 20mm M61 cannon, the F-16A as seen here has been continually upgraded and made much more capable. In USAF service it is now used as a fighter-bomber rather than in the air superiority mission.

Below: One of the first block F-16A Fighting Falcons was used in 1981 for initial evaluation trials of the Hughes AIM-120 Amraam, a fire and forget missile which is currently in the course of replacing the AIM-7 Sparrow. The new weapon will be carried by the F-16C/D, which has the far more capable APG-68 radar and upgraded avionics to match the new weapon.

Development: Originally intended as an austere lightweight fighter to complement the F-15 Eagle in a hi-lo technology fighter mix, the F-16 was designed for agility before all else. The study group that had defined the USAF Lightweight Fighter (LWF) requirements had concluded that in any future war, air combat would, despite the availability of medium range missiles, quickly come down to visual range where manoeuvrability was at a premium and numbers would count. The F-15 was proving unaffordable in the numbers required, and the idea was to supplement the highly capable Eagle force with an agile close combat fighter.

Having won the USAF LWF competition, the F-16 was selected as an F-104 replacement for four European nations; Belgium, Denmark, The Netherlands, and Norway. But Belgium also needed an aircraft with the ability to deliver tactical nuclear weapons, with the result that the production F-16A emerged as rather larger and heavier, more expensive, and certainly less austere than the original preproduction aircraft. The F-16B, a conversion trainer with two seats, was also put into production.

Remarkably manoeuvrable, the F-16 startled onlookers during its international public debut at Le Bourget in 1977 with 8g sustained turns. The first service aircraft to combine relaxed stability with quadruplex fly-by-wire (FBW) with no

Right: An F-16A of the 8th FW 'Wolf Pack', based at Kunsan in South Korea. The F-16A is the most agile of the breed, as later variants suffered from creeping weight growth only partially redressed by more powerful engines. A specially modified F-16A with improved radar is used for the air defence of the United States.

Above: A Korean-based 8th FW F-16A rotates before takeoff. This unit has since been re-equipped with the more capable F-16C/D, with the Westinghouse APG-68 radar. The South Korean Air Force also operates 40 F-16C/Ds in the air defence role. The primary North Korean air threat aircraft is the MiG-29 Fulcrum, which has a performance comparable to that of the F-16. Nearly 4,000 F-16s have been ordered to date.

Left: The first aircraft in service to combine relaxed stability with FBW, the F-16 has many radical features, not the least of which are a sidestick controller in place of the conventional central control column, and a steeply raked seat to increase the pilot's 'g' tolerance levels. The chin intake was found to offer the best solution to disturbed airflow in sideslip.

Above: The demonstration F-16C flies past at low speed and high alpha, as evidenced by the smoke trails from the wingtip pods.

mechanical backup, it was also radical in having a sidestick force transducer control column, a steeply raked seat to increase the pilot's resistance to g forces, and a single piece frameless canopy of heavy acrylic to give near perfect all-round visibility. The fuselage was tailored tightly around the engine and cockpit, while the moderately swept wings featured automatic variable camber. Leading edge root extensions caused vortices which energised the stagnant boundary layer air away from the wing surfaces, delaying the onset of separation and stalls at high angles of attack. A chin inlet, situated beneath the cockpit, had been selected as the position most resistant to disturbed airflow during manoeuvres involving sideslip.

The original F-16 was a fairly basic aircraft, making use of traditional materials and methods, the one exception being the FBW system, which saved an enormous amount of weight by eliminating hydraulics. No composites were used and very little titanium. The Westinghouse APG-66 radar had a modest performance and air-to-air armament consisted of a single 20mm six barrel Vulcan cannon with 511 rounds, plus two AIM-9 Sidewinder heat-seeking missiles carried on wingtip rails.

One of the LWF requirements had been for combat endurance, and the F-16A was given a fuel fraction of 0.30. It had been calculated that much less than this made a fighter fuel critical, while much more incurred a weight and performance penalty. The endurance of the F-16A is good, and it rarely has to

Left: The F-16B is a fully combat capable two seater conversion trainer, as is the F-16D. The second seat is shoe-horned in at the cost of reduced fuel capacity.

Below: A closeup of the unique single-piece canopy, which gives an unsurpassed all-round view. The transparency is very thick, and has a distinctive gold tint. The pilot has a limited movement sidestick controller by his right hand which provides control inputs to the Fly-by-Wire (FBW) system.

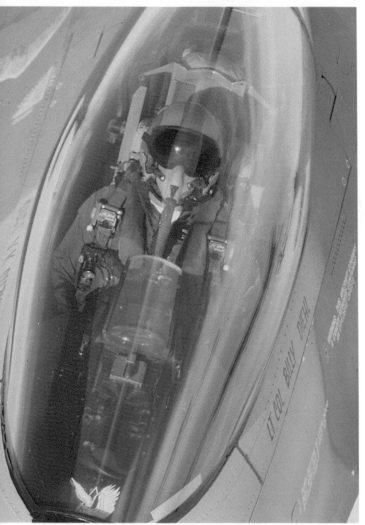

break off combat due to fuel shortage. This is not entirely true of the F-16B, which although fully combat capable in every other way, has 1,151lb (522kg) less fuel to accommodate the second seat, which amounts to 17 per cent of the total internal fuel load.

But although combat persistence in endurance terms is good, two Sidewinders are insufficient, and the F-16A could very quickly expend its weapons. The European customers also found that its adverse weather capability is inadequate.

A multi-stage improvement programme (MSIP) was put in hand, and this resulted in the F-16C and D. These are fitted with the far more capable APG-68 radar and advanced cockpit displays, have provision for the future use of AIM-120A

Below: Armed with AGM-88A HARM missiles, F-16s combine with F-4Gs to form hunter/killer teams in the Wild Weasel mission.

Amraam missiles, and carry a greater payload. Block 40 aircraft, the first of which was delivered in January 1989, are kitted out for night and adverse weather operations. Referred to as Night Falcons, they carry two Lantirn navigation and targeting pods, while the flight control system is digital rather than analogue.

Other variants in service are the 'specially configured' F-16A ADF, and the F-16N. The former is really a modified F-16C optimised for the air defence of the USA, but has the APG-66 radar, upgraded to handle AIM-7 Sparrow or Amraam missiles. Weapons load is six AIM-7s or Amraams, or six AIM-9s. A quick reaction inertial system permits a short scramble time, and the cockpit displays of the F-16C are retained.

Below: A Nellis-based F-16 of the 474th FW releases slicks over the bombing range. The F-16 has been increasingly used as a bomb truck.

Below: The first Block 40 F-16C Night Falcon, seen here carrying AGM-65 Maverick missiles and Lantirn targeting pods.

Above: F-16Cs were extensively used in the Gulf War. Seen here in Saudi Arabia, this 363rd FW F-16C is normally based at Shaw AFB.

The F-16N is an austere variant used for adversary training by the USN. It carries no weapons; just a tethered Sidewinder and an Air Combat Manoeuvring Instrumentation (ACMI) pod.

Finally there is the RF-16, a dedicated reconnaissance variant to replace the RF-4C Phantom. This carries an Advanced Tactical Air Reconnaissance System (ATARS) pod ventrally, which combines electro-optical sensors with IR line scanners. The RF-16 is scheduled to achieve IOC in 1993.

The F-16 has seen considerable action over the years. Israeli F-16s are credited with shooting down 44 Syrian aircraft in the Beka'a Valley action in 1982, while Pakistani F-16s accounted for several Afghan aircraft after border violations in the late 'eighties. But notwithstanding its undoubted close air combat capabilities, the USAF has increasingly used it as a bomb truck, and this was its role in the Gulf War of 1991. A total of 249 USAF F-16s were deployed to the Gulf, and flew 13,450 sorties against such diverse targets as airfields, chemical production facilities, Scud missile launchers and ground units. In all, 2,459 F-16s of all types are planned for the USAF by 1999.

Below: A thirsty F-16C takes on fuel over Saudi Arabia before departing for hostile skies, loaded with Rockeye CBUs.

General Dynamics F-111

F-111A, D, E, F, G, EF-111A

Origin: General Dynamics Corporation, Fort Worth, Texas; (EF-111A) Grumman Aerospace Corporation, Bethpage, New York.

Type: (A, D, E, F, G) all-weather attack aircraft, (EF-111A) EW aircraft.

Engines: Two P&W TF30 afterburning turbofans as follows: (A, C) 18,500lb (8,390kg) TF30-3, (D, E) 19,600lb (8,891kg) TF30-9, (G) 20,350lb (9,231kg) TF30-7, (F) 25,100lb (11,385kg) TF30-100, (EF-111A) 20,500lb (9,300kg) TF30-109.

Dimensions: Span (fully spread) (A, D, E, F, EF) 63ft (19.2m), (G) 70ft (21.34m), (fully swept) (A, D, E, F, EF) 31ft 11½in (9.74m), (G) 70ft 11in (10.34m); length (except EF) 73ft 6in (22.4m), (EF) 77ft 1½in (23.51m); wing area (A, D, E, F, EF, gross, 16°) 525 sq ft (48.77m²).

Weights: Empty (A) 46,172lb (20,943kg), (D) 49,090lb (22,267kg), (E) about 47,000lb (21,319kg), (EF) 53,418lb (24,230kg), (F) 47,481lb (21,537kg), (G) close to 50,000lb (22,680kg); loaded (A) 91,500lb (41,500kg), (D, E) 92,500lb (41,954kg), (F) 100,000lb (45,360kg), (G) 114,300lb (51,846kg), (EF) 87,478lb (39,680kg).

Performance: Max speed at altitude, clean; (A, D, E) Mach 2.2; (F) Mach 2.5; (G) Mach 2; (EF) Mach 1.75; low level penetration speed (all) about 496kt (991km/hr); initial climb rate (all) 30-40,000ft/min (152-203m/sec); service ceiling at combat weight (A) 51,000ft (15,544m), (F) 60,000ft (18,287m), (EF) 54,700ft (16,672m); range with max int. fuel (A, D) 2,750nm (5,096km), (F) 2,540nm (4,707km), (EF) 2,157nm (3,998km); take-off run (A) 4,000ft (1,219m); (F) 3,000ft (914m); (G) 4,700ft (1,432m); (EF) 3,250ft (991m).

Armament: Internal weapons bay for two B43 special weapons or (D, F) one B43 and one 20mm M61 cannon; six underwing pylons, the four inboard swivelling, the two outers fixed and usable only at minimum wing sweep for maximum external load of 31,500lb (14,288kg), (G only) provision for up to six AGM-131A SRAM IIs, or conventional weapons; (EF) none.

History: First flight 21 December 1964; service delivery (A) June 1967, (EF) July 1981, (G) 1990.

Users: ACC, USAFE.

Above: An F-111F with wings at intermediate sweep loaded with LGBs and equipped with the Pave Tack laser designation system.

Right: The F-111 carries a tremendous punch, as shown by this 366 FW aircraft releasing no less than 24 Mk 82 slicks over the range.

Development: If the United States Air Force in Europe had ever been called upon to fly retaliatory attack missions against the Soviet Union following a first strike from the East, the principal tactical air weapon used would have been the General Dynamics F-111. Day or night, sunshine or snow, nearly 200 of these remarkable aircraft flying from airfields in the UK would have undertaken low-level bombing missions against targets in the western USSR and the bordering Warsaw Pact countries. Together with the Tornado, the F-111 was the only aircraft capable of this type of operation available to NATO. Yet in its infancy this advanced design seemed destined never to overcome a whole string of problems which attracted the attention of the world's press and called into question the political decisions that forced the programme through to a conclusion.

Above: A brooding dusk shot of an F-111, showing its side by side cockpit configuration, which aids crew co-operation.

Backing the TFX (Tactical Fighter Experimental) programme, the US Department of Defense directed that one design was to fulfil all the fighter and attack needs of the Air Force, Navy and Marine Corps, despite the different requirements of these services. General Dynamics won the contract, and the prototype F-111 flew on 21 December 1964. Serious development problems followed, involving an increase in weight, excessive aerodynamic drag and engine inlet difficulties, compounded by a number of in-flight structural failures. The Navy F-111B programme was cancelled in 1968 and an order for 24 F-111Cs for the Royal Australian Air Force was temporarily shelved until urgent modifications were incorporated in the aircraft; delivery of these would be made in 1973.

Below: Off to war! Armed with GBU-15 precision glide bombs, a trio of F-111s sets off in search of targets in Iraq in 1991.

Below: An F-111F delivers its load of retarded bombs at low level. The retardation ensures that the aircraft is well clear of the explosions.

To prove that the F-111A could function effectively in the attack role (the fighter task had been impossible to meet because of the aircraft's poor power-to-weight ratio), the USAF deployed six F-111As to Thailand in mid-1968 for operations against North Vietnam. The loss of three of these aircraft shortly after their arrival clouded what was in fact a vindication of the GD design. Courageous Air Force crews pioneered terrain-following missions across unknown country during the blackest of nights, often in the worst weather that South-East Asia could provide, flying over hills, round mountains and along steep-sided valleys, holding a steady 200ft (90m) above the ground at high sub-sonic speed, and finally precision-bombing a target to within feet of the aiming point. The crew, snug in their jettisonable cockpit capsules, would then return to more hospitable environments, having caught the ground defences unawares and having been undetected by the early warning radars ringing the northern borders. In 1972 an F-111 detachment returned to South East Asia and operated with great success.

In all, 141 F-111As were built. This was the model later selected for conversion into the EF-111A electronic warfare variant by Grumman, who rebuilt 42 F-111As as Ravens. Grumman were also responsible for the navalisation of the abortive F-111B carrier fighter, the failure of which resulted in the development of the F-14 Tomcat. Next came the F-111C for the Royal Australian Air Force, while the next variant to enter USAF service was the F-111E, of which 96 were built. This had the original -3 engines, matched to the Triple Plow II inlet. The 96 F-111Ds

Above: Four Paveway II laser-guided bombs hang under the wings of this F-111F from the 48th FW; under the fuselage is a Pave Tack pod.

Below: An F-111F of the 48th FW based at RAF Lakenheath, UK, pictured in December 1982 and carrying a practice-bomb dispenser.

were produced out of sequence, with more powerful -9 engines and Triple Plow II inlets. The APQ-130 radar and APQ-128 terrain-following radar replaced the original APQ-113 and APQ-110, and avionics generally were updated.

What is generally recognised to be the best of the breed is the F-111F, which equipped the 48th TFW at Lakenheath, UK. Two 25,100lb thrust TF30 turbofans replace less powerful engines, but the key to this aircraft's success is the addition of the Pave Tack system. This is located in the belly of the F-111F and provides a day/night, all-weather capability to acquire, track, designate and hit surface targets using electro-optical, infra-red or laser guided weapons. To provide an anti-runway capability, the French Durandal, parachute retarded, rocket boosted bomb was acquired in large numbers for the F-111F, which could carry up to twelve of these weapons. The minimum release height is, however, rather on the high side, making the aircraft very vulnerable to ground fire. It was noticeable that no attempt to use Durandal was made during the Gulf War, almost certainly for this reason. F-111E/Fs based in the UK also carried AIM-9L Sidewinders to provide a credible self defence capability, plus an ALQ-131 ECM pod under the rear fuselage. The FB-111A, of which 67 were built, was developed specifically as a strategic nuclear weapons delivery system for SAC. It featured a larger wing with greater area, more hardpoints, increased fuel capacity, a strengthened structure, beefed up landing gear to allow greater operating weights, and a comprehensive nav/attack system derived from that of the F-111D. Weapons load was up to six SRAM or six special weapons. In 1988, the decision was taken to modify surviving FB-111As to fly tactical missions as F-111Gs, although the SRAM capability is retained. The conversion programme, which mainly concerns avionics and systems, is scheduled to be complete by 1994.

The final variant is the rather exotic EF-111A Raven. When the USAF sought a successor for the EB-66 electronic warfare aircraft, the only contender in sight was the EA-6 Prowler, operated by the USN. This lacked both performance and range, needed a four man crew and was very costly. The solution was to take the least potent F-111A, adapt it to carry the ALQ-99 EW suite of the Prowler, modified and largely automated for two-man operation. This was duly done, to produce the ALQ-99E. Most of the black boxes are mounted in what used to be the weapons bay, and the original TF30-3 turbofans were replaced by the more powerful -109s. A digital upgrade programme began in 1989, to provide faster processing and even more capability.

Left: Distinguishable by its pale grey finish and large fin-top pod, the EF-111A Raven is a dedicated jamming aircraft adapted from the F-111A.

Below: Just one of the many electronic countermeasures that the Raven can employ against enemy radar is this snowstorm rendering the screen unreadable.

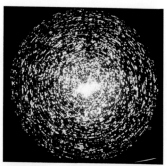

Above: The cockpit of the Raven, showing the pilot's position at left, and the Electronic Warfare Officer's position at the right.

F-111E/Fs carried out the raid on Libya in April 1986, operating from bases in the UK, and detouring right around the Iberian Peninsula with the aid of flight refuelling. A force of 27 F-111Es and 66 F-111Fs took part in the Gulf War in 1991, flying more than 4,000 sorties during which just one aircraft was slightly damaged. Main targets were chemical, biological and nuclear facilities, plus airfields and command centres. Also in theatre were 18 EF-111As, which averaged 50 missions apiece, supporting attack aircraft by jamming and degrading the Iraqi detection, command and control systems.

Grumman A-6 Intruder/ EA-6 Prowler

A-6E Intruder, EA-6B Prowler, KA-6D

Origin: Grumman Aerospace, Bethpage, New York.
Type: (all) carrier based, (A-6E) two-seater all-weather attack aircraft, (EA-6B) four-seater EW aircraft, (KA-6D) two-seat tanker.
Engines: (A-6E, KA-6D) two J52-P-8B turbojets each rated at 9,300lb (4,218kg); (EA-6B) two J52-P-408 turbojets each rated at 11,200lb (5,080kg).
Dimensions: Span (all) 53ft (16.15m); length (A-6E, KA-6D) 54ft 9in (16.69m), (EA-6B) 59ft 10in (18.24m); height (A-6E, KA-6D) 16ft 2in (4.93m); (EA-6B) 16ft 3in (4.95m).
Weights: Empty (A-6E) 26,746lb (12,132kg), (EA-6B) 32,162lb (14,588kg), (KA-6D) 26,600lb (12,066kg); max take-off weight (A-6E) 58,600lb (26,581kg), (EA-6B) 65,000lb (29,483kg) (KA-6D) 53,500lb (24,268kg); max carrier landing weight (A-6E, KA-6D) 36,000lb (16,329kg), (EA-6B) 45,500lb (20,638kg).
Performance: Max speed at sea level (A-6E, KA-6D) 560kt (1,037km/hr), (EA-6B) 530kt (982km/hr); initial climb rate (A-6E, KA-6D) 7,620ft/min (39m/sec), (EA-6B) 10,030ft/min (51m/sec), service ceiling (A-6E, KA-6D) 42,400ft (12,923m), (EA-6B) 38,000ft (11,582m), range with full combat load (A-6E, KA-6D) 878nm (1,627km), (EA-6B) 955nm (1,769km); ferry range (A-6E, KA-6D) 2,818nm (5,222km), (EA-6B) 2,085nm (3,861km).
Armament: (A-6E) five stores pylons each rated at 3,600lb (1,633kg). Wide variety of iron and smart bombs, four sea mines, four each AGM-65 Maverick, AGM-84 Harpoon, or AGM-88 HARM missiles, or one SLAM, two AIM-9L or P Sidewinder AAMs. Provision has also been made for Amraam. (KA-6D) none. (EA-6B) up to six AGM-88A HARM anti-radar missiles.
History: First flight (YA2F-1) 19 April 1960, (KA-6D) 23 May 1966, (EA-6B) 25 May 1968, (A-6E) 10 November 1970.
Users: USN, USMC.

Above: The small ball turret under the nose is the TRAM sensor, now fitted to all A-6E Intruders as standard.

Development: As the Navy's primary medium attack aircraft, the A-6 Intruder has proved itself to be just about the best of the world's carrier-based bombers. It can hardly be called the most modern of combat aircraft, however, since it was conceived in the late 1950s and entered US Navy service in February 1963, more than two decades ago. It then played a significant role in South-East Asia, operating in the Gulf of Tonkin against enemy targets in the darkest of nights and the dirtiest of weather when the only other types likely to be about were the modest number of USAF-operated F-111As.

Because of the space problem on aircraft carriers, the Intruder's size was kept small, with the result that all ordnance had to be mounted externally, thus incurring certain drag penalties. However, the aircraft's amazing ability to find and hit targets in weather too bad for most other aircraft to operate, combined

Below: A mixed bag of weaponry is carried by this A-6E, the carriage of AGM-88A HARM missiles identifying a SWIP-improved aircraft.

Above: Like all carrier-based aircraft, the Intruder features wing folding to reduce the amount of deck/hangar space it occupies.

with its prowess as a bomb truck, more than compensated for any drawbacks.

The current Intruder/Prowler family consists of the A-6E Intruder all-weather interdiction/attack aircraft, the KA-6D, an air refuelling tanker variant with weapons capability deleted, and the EA-6B Prowler dedicated EW aircraft, which also carries HARM missiles for defence suppression. A small number of less capable EA-6As remain in service with the USMC.

Radar carried in the nose is the Norden APQ-148, a multi-mode type which combines terrain avoidance, ground mapping, detection, tracking, and identification of fixed or moving targets. This is augmented by a Target Recognition Attack Multisensor (TRAM), mounted in a ball turret under the nose. TRAM incorporates Forward Looking Infra-Red (FLIR) to give TV quality images of targets at night, a laser ranger/designator, and a laser spot tracker. Early A-6Es did not have TRAM, but a retrofit programme saw them all so equipped by 1988. The most recent update is the Systems/Weapons Improvement Program(SWIP), which commenced in August 1987 with new build aircraft. Retrofits to existing aircraft started in November 1988. SWIP provides a significant stand-off weapons capability, allowing the A-6E to use the Harpoon anti-shipping missile, the HARM anti-radar missile and the Maverick air-to-surface missile (in both laser and IR homing configurations).

The latest advance is the Integrated Defense Avionics Program (IDAP). This

Below: A good view of the TRAM turret in this shot of an A-6E being 'fed to the cat'. The nosewheel launch bar is already engaged.

Above: The KA-6D is the tanker variant of the Intruder. It uses a refuelling drogue rather than the flying boom favoured by the USAF.

consists of active S-band radar coverage through 360° to detect incoming missiles, which will be automatically countered with a combination of chaff, flares, and towed decoys. Three towed decoys are carried, reeled out from the aircraft on a cable to where they provide a better alternative target at a safe distance astern. Also part of IDAP is a wing fillet modification to increase the carrier recovery weight by 2,000lb (907kg), thereby ensuring that expensive smart munitions do not have to be jettisoned before landing back.

Two Intruder variants that never entered service were the A-6F Intruder II and the A-6G. The former featured improved digital avionics, including inverse-gain synthetic aperture radar processing and Doppler beam sharpening techniques; both aimed at improving target identification. Air-to-air capability was to be included, using Amraam, while extra power was given by two F404-GE-404 unaugmented turbofans. The A-6G was a toned down F, with all the avionics upgrades but powered by the same turbojets as the EA-6B. Budgetary

Below: When extra tanker capacity is needed, the A-6E can use the buddy refuelling pack, as seen here topping up a Corsair II.

Above: An EA-6B electronic warfare variant overflies the desert during the Gulf War. Most ECM kit is carried in five pods.

restrictions caused the cancellation of both types in 1988/89.

Modified from early A-6 variants, the KA-6D tanker first flew in May 1966 and since then has provided an invaluable air refuelling capability. Originally the KA-6D retained a limited attack capability, but this has since been deleted.

The EA-6B Prowler is rather larger than the Intruder from which it was developed, with an extended front section to house two extra ECM specialists. The other external difference is a large pod on the top of the fin, which houses detection equipment. Current ECM fit is the ALQ-99F system carried in five pods, two under each wing and the other beneath the fuselage, each with two jamming transmitters. The latest update is the ADVCAP EA-6B, which carries HARM and the Lockheed/Sanders ALQ-149 communications jammer.

Early A-6s were active throughout the Vietnam War, and A-6Es, KA-6Ds and EA-6Bs have been used over Lebanon, Libya, Grenada, Panama, and finally during the Gulf War, in which they played a distinguished part. But the design is now very old, and A-6Es were to have been replaced by the A-12 Avenger II. Cancellation of the A-12 has forced the extension of their active life, and Intruders will have to be around for a while yet.

Grumman F-14 Tomcat

F-14A, A +, D

Origin: Grumman Aerospace, Bethpage, New York.
Type: Two seat carrier-based interceptor.
Engines: (A) Two 20,900lb (9,480kg) thrust P&W TF30-414A afterburning turbofans, (A +, D) two 27,080lb (12,283kg) thrust GE F110-400 afterburning turbofans.
Dimensions: Span (all) swept 38ft 2in (11.60m), spread 64ft 2in (19.52m); length (A) 62ft 8in (19.1m) (A +, D) 61ft 11in (18.87m); height (all) 16ft (4.88m).
Weights: Empty (A) 39,921lb (18,110kg), (D) 41,780lb (18,951kg); loaded (six AIM-54s) (A) 69,700lb (31,656kg), (D) 73,038lb (33,130kg); max (all) 74,349lb (33,724kg).
Performance: Max speed at altitude (A) Mach 2.31, (D) Mach 1.88; at sea

level (all) Mach 1.2; interception radius with Mach 1.5 dash speed (A) 134nm (248km), (A+, D) 217nm (402km); time on station at 150nm (278km) (A) 91min (A+, D) 122min; initial climb rate (A) 30,000ft/min (152m/sec) plus, (A+, D) 45,000ft/min (229m/sec) plus; service ceiling (A) 50,000ft (15,239m), (A+, D) 53,000ft (16,154m).

Armament: (All) One 20mm M61 Vulcan cannon with 675 rounds, max eight missiles in any permutation from six AIM-54 Phoenix, six AIM-7F Sparrow or AIM-120A Amraam, and four AIM-9L or P Sidewinders. The F-14A has never carried air-to-surface weaponry operationally, but the A+ and D may well be cleared to do so in the early 'nineties.

History: (A) first flight 21 December 1970, service entry 14 October 1972, operational carrier deployment September 1974; (A+, D) first flight 29 September 1986, service entry November 1989.

User: USN.

Below: F-14A Tomcat with its maximum load of six AIM-54 Phoenix missiles. More usually a mix of AIM-54, AIM-7 and AIM-9 is carried.

Development: Designed as a fleet air defence interceptor, with an unparalleled long range kill capability allied to great agility and high performance, the Tomcat still ranks among the world's best despite its age. Even so, it has had surprisingly few chances of demonstrating its worth in combat compared to other fighters. Several F-14A and F-14A + squadrons took part in the Gulf War of 1991, but opportunities for air combat were virtually non-existent, and the only kill of this conflict was an Iraqi helicopter. On the other hand, it has clashed with Libyan Arab Air Force fighters over the Mediterranean on two occasions, and each time acquitted itself honourably.

The first occasion was the Gulf of Sidra incident in August 1981, when two F-14As of VF-41 Black Aces were intercepted by two Su-22 Fitters, one of which launched a missile in their general direction. The combat lasted less than 90 seconds. As the Fitters passed them, the F-14s swung in behind and launched Sidewinders, sending both Libyan aircraft into the sea. The next clash took place in January 1989, when two Libyan MiG-23s were downed over the Mediterranean after making apparently hostile moves against two patrolling Tomcats from the carrier *John F. Kennedy*. The Gulf War of 1991 saw the new F-14A + in action for the first time, but this conflict was disappointing for the Tomcat drivers, as lack of combat opportunity meant that their only air-to-air victory was the previously mentioned helicopter.

The variable-sweep wings are computer-controlled and can move automatically between 20° and 68°; fully swept, they give the F-14 greater acceleration in combat, and when fully extended they allow take-offs in less than 1,000ft (300m) and landings in 2,000ft (600m) at low air speeds. To further improve its flying characteristics, the F-14 has small retractable glove vanes in the fixed leading edge of the wings (a unique feature of the design), and these normally deploy automatically above Mach 1.

The Tomcat's weapon system is built around the impressive AWG-9 radar and the Hughes AIM-54 Phoenix long-range air-to-air missile. With its 132lb (60kg) explosive warhead, capable of knocking down the largest of aircraft, the Phoenix has demonstrated its operational capability over more than 150 firings, destroying drones simulating a range of targets including Soviet Backfire bombers and Foxbat fighters at heights varying between 50ft (15m) and 80,000ft (24,400m), at speeds of up to Mach 2.8 and at ranges of more than 100 miles (160km). The radar/missile system is also capable of engaging up to six targets at the same time, and tests have shown an 80 per cent kill rate for this type of attack.

Tomcats fulfil the fighter-cover role for the majority of the US Navy's attack carriers, each ship normally having a complement of two 12-aircraft squadrons. At sea the Tomcats normally operate in pairs under the control of an E-2C Hawkeye early warning aircraft and usually undertake any one of three types of mission: air cover for a task force (FORCAP); air cover for attack aircraft in enemy airspace (TARCAP); and barrier defence against retaliatory air attacks (BARCAP). Although each aircraft can carry up to six Phoenix missiles, the routine armament for most sorties consists of two examples each of the AIM-9 Sidewinder, AIM-7 Sparrow and AIM-54 Phoenix which, combined with the cannon, gives a potent warload for most situations. Two or three F-14As on each carrier can now carry

Above: An important element in carrier operations is the air refuelling tanker. A KA-6D of VA-35 aboard *Nimitz* pumps fuel into one of two Tomcats of VF-41 'Black Aces' complete in toned-down markings.

Left: The ultimate in lo-viz markings is shown on this F-14A of VF-101 'Grim Reapers'. In 1990, brighter unit and other markings started to make a comeback.

Below: The hot end of a Tomcat, showing the variable outlet nozzles and between them the unique beaver tail. The widely separated engine pods give extra keel area and contribute to directional stability.

Above: Sparrows and Sidewinders are the more normal weapons fit, as seen here in this shot taken during Operation Desert Shield.

Below: A handful of Tomcats on each carrier are wired to carry the TARPs tactical reconnaissance pod, as seen here on the centreline.

TARPS (Tactical Airborne Reconnaissance Pod System); a total of 49 aircraft have this capability. The pod houses cameras for forward-oblique, panoramic or vertical shots, and an infra-red scanner; it is located under the rear fuselage where it sterilises the two rear missile hardpoints.

The F-14A was originally intended as an interim type, pending the arrival of the F-14B powered by F401-P-400 turbofans. This was cancelled due to lack of funds, and the next variant proposed was the F-14C, with improved avionics. This also fell by the wayside. The original engines were the greatest weakness of the F-14A, being sensitive to disturbed airflow, unreliable, and lacking sufficient thrust. The AWG-9 radar had also become dated over the years and it was obvious that something better was needed in both departments.

The first step was the F-14A +, which differed from the A model primarily in having two F110-GE-400 engines. These gave far more thrust, carefree handling, and better specific fuel consumption, giving enhanced performance across the board, including the ability to launch from the carrier in military power at quite high weights. The inlet ramp was rescheduled to handle the greater mass airflow, while the engine, being considerably shorter than the TF30, needed an extension to fit. The F-14A + first flew on 29 September 1986, and entered service in November 1989.

Meanwhile the F-14D had commenced development in 1984. This included a full avionics upgrade, with the Hughes APG-71 radar and digital processing, which not only gave extra modes and greater capability, but provided non-cooperative target recognition. The Northrop TCS was retained, and a GE IRST fitted, both in pods beneath the nose. Unfortunately, lack of funds once more intruded and only a handful of F-14Ds were built, although the conversion of the F-14A into A + continues.

Lockheed F-117A

F-117A

Origin: Lockheed Advanced Development Projects, (The Skunk Works), Burbank, California.
Type: Single-seat attack and defence suppression aircraft.
Engines: Two 10,800lb (4,899kg) General Electric F404-F1D2 unaugmented turbofans.
Dimensions: Span 43ft 4in (13.20m); length 65ft 11in (20.08m); height 12ft 5in (3.78m); wing area est. 880sq ft (81.75m²).
Weights: Empty 29,500lb (13,381kg); max take-off 52,500lb (23.814kg).
Performance: Max speed Mach 0.9; unrefuelled range c1,100nm (2,038km); endurance (with inflight refuelling) 12 hours.
Armament: 'Full range of USAF tactical fighter ordnance'; two 2,000lb (970kg) BLU-109, GBU-24, GBU-27 LGBs, or two AGM-65 Maverick carried internally; max load 5,000lb (2,268kg).
History: First flight XST proof of concept aircraft 1978; F-117A 18 June 1981; 59th and final delivery Autumn 1989.
User: USAF (ACC).

Development: One of the most remarkable things about the F-117A was that in an open society such as that of the United States, an advanced combat aircraft could have been designed, built and entered service in fair numbers, and operated for several years, all in conditions of almost complete secrecy. There were of course rumours about a so-called F-19; and many artists impressions, all of them highly inaccurate, found their way into print, which aided security by muddying the waters further.

The Nighthawk, as it is unofficially known, started life in 1973 as a design study codenamed *Have Blue*, the object of which was to determine to what degree an aircraft could be made invisible to radar and IR detection systems. The result was two Experimental Stealth Tactical (XST) prototypes which first flew in mid-1977. Results being satisfactory, the decision to develop a production aircraft was taken about one year later, and this first flew from Groom Lake in June 1981.

The F-117A was in appearance like nothing else in the air. It was made up of sharp angles and flat surfaces, without a curve in sight. The idea behind this shaping was that where radar impulses could not be absorbed, they should be deflected away from the emitter, and the angles were carefully calculated

Below: The angular appearance of the F-117A is due to the need to deflect hostile radar emissions away from the receiver.

to do this. The skin was largely of aluminium, although titanium was used around the hot end, coated in Radar Absorbent Material (RAM) optimised to soak up energy at the wavelengths commonly used by radars. The two biggest radar reflectors on an aircraft are the engine compressor faces, and the cockpit. The former were set above the wing surfaces and screened with grilles carefully spaced to defeat radar energy, while the latter was given a heavy, angular framed canopy which conformed to the overall shape of the fuselage. The small flat transparencies were given a conductive coating to prevent radar emissions actually entering the cockpit. The view from the window is poor, but the stealth advantages more than compensate. Infra-red was the other means of detection to be guarded against, and this was done mainly by flat slot efflux ducts which not only partially shield the hot nozzles, but expel the exhaust gases in a thin sheet, which quickly cools as it mixes with the surrounding air.

Tremendous attention to detail is apparent in the shaping of the F-117A, with angular profiles being used even on the weapons bay and landing gear doors, to say nothing of the air data probes on the nose. The actual radar cross-section of the aircraft is classified, but is believed to be about that of a medium-sized bird.

The overall angular shape, resembling nothing so much as a shallow inverted salt cellar, is most unaerodynamic, and could easily qualify it for the soubriquet of 'Vortexmaster'. Nor did the exceptionally sharp leading edge sweep of 67½° and the equally sharply swept butterfly tail, add to its intrinsic handling qualities. It has been stated that modern technology could make the Statue of Liberty fly, although how well was not revealed. Something along these lines was needed for the F-117A. Digital quadruplex fly-by-wire was essential, and even this was beset by difficulties in the early stages. The 'Wobblin Goblin' epithet, strongly denied by the Air Force, dated back to the days when the aircraft was so unstable that it did 'everything but fall on its tail when it was standing on its wheels', as one test pilot stated in 1991. This has since been cured, and it is now reported to handle quite nicely.

The first operational aircraft arrived in 1982, and IOC was achieved by the 4450th Test Squadron in October 1983. Virtually all flying was done at night in order to preserve secrecy, including a new pilot's first solo on type. Unlike most other tactical aircraft, there is no two seater conversion trainer. This lasted until November 1988, when the wraps were finally taken off and some daylight flying began.

Above: Stealth over-rode all other considerations in the design of the Black Jet; including the view from the cockpit.

Below: From any angle the F-117A looks sinister, its pyramidal section contrasting sharply with a completely flat underside.

Above: A thirsty F-117A pulls alongside a tanker. It uses the standard USAF flying boom and receptacle refuelling method.

The F-117A is a one-mission aeroplane, optimised for precision attack against high value targets at night. It is reported to carry a high precision INS and GPS for accurate navigation, a FLIR sensor in front of the windshield and a retractable FLIR/laser designator ventrally. Radar does not appear to feature, which is hardly surprising.

Combat debut came in Decmber 1989 when two bombs were dropped near an army barracks in Panama, but the real test came in the Gulf War of 1991. In this conflict, F-117s deployed nonstop from the USA to bases in Saudi Arabia, from which they flew more than 1,250 sorties. In a true test of combat capability, they penetrated Iraqi air defence systems undetected and made precision attacks on command and control centres and other high value targets. The fact that they could avoid detection meant that target identification was not a hurried matter; essential to meet the stringent Rules of Engagement enforced by coalition leaders to minimise civilian casualties. Finally a system whereby all aircraft in a given target area could release their weapons within a few seconds of each other ensured that the Iraqi air defences were not alerted in time to put up a barrage of gunfire until the F-117As were already egressing. The result was that accurate attacks could be made, collateral damage was minimised, and not one F-117A was even scratched.

Below: Two F-117As on the ramp outside their hardened shelters in Saudi Arabia. The flattened engine nozzles can just be made out.

Lockheed F-22A

F-22A

Origin: Lockheed/Boeing/General Dynamics.
Type: Single seater air superiority fighter.
Engines: Two 35,000lb (15,876kg) P&W F119-100 augmented turbofans with vectoring thrust nozzles.
Dimensions: Span 43ft (13.11m); length 64ft 2½in (19.57m); height 17ft 8½in (5.39m); wing area 830sq ft (77.11m²).
Weights: Empty 34,000lb (15,422kg); normal take-off 62,000lb (28,123kg).
Performance: Max speed cMach 2.5 at altitude, Mach 1.21 S/L; sustained supercruise speed Mach 1.4 to 1.5; ceiling c70,000ft (21,335m); combat radius c800nm (1,482km).
Armament: One 20mm cannon, four AIM-120A Amraam and four AIM-9 Sidewinder missiles carried internally.
History: First flight YF-22A 29 September 1990, contract award April 1991, first production F-22 scheduled for 1995, IOC 2002, production 648 aircraft by 2012.
User: USAF (ACC), USN (NATF variant) possibly.

Development: By 1980, the F-15 was widely acknowledged as the world's finest fighter, and this state of affairs seemed likely to persist for many years after. By the end of the century, however, despite more powerful engines and improved weapons systems, it would become increasingly obsolete. What would be needed was a new fighter capable of operating in the face of advanced air defence systems, without incurring an unacceptable loss rate. This problem was to be attacked on two fronts; speed and stealth.

Maximum speeds have been largely irrelevant over the past three decades. They take forever to reach, and if you ever do, the fuel warning light comes on and you have to slow down. At the same time, it has always been true that an appreciable speed advantage gives the initiative in combat. Therefore the really important speed parameter is sustained cruise.

The ability to detect without being detected is also vital in air combat and both qualities of stealth and speed combine to defeat surface-to-air missiles. All this enables a fighter possessing them to operate over hostile territory at high altitudes with relative impunity. It was therefore obvious that the next generation air superiority fighter would need to possess both sustained speed and low observability. Sustained speed was defined as the ability to cruise at supersonic speeds for extended periods without using afterburner. At the same time, neither requirement was to be met at the expense of air combat manoeuvrability. Such was the baseline for the USAF Advanced Tactical Fighter (ATF) programme.

Conceptual design studies were awarded to seven companies in September 1983. This was followed by development contracts awarded in October 1986 to Lockheed, teamed with Boeing and General Dynamics; and Northrop, teamed with McDonnell Douglas. Both contractors were to produce two flying prototypes for evaluation, each of which used P&W YF119 and GE YF120 turbofans.

The first contender to fly was Northrop's YF-23A, on 27 August 1990. It was followed into the air by the YF-22A on 29 September of that year. In appearance they were considerably different, the Northrop fighter's trapezoidal wing and steeply canted ruddervators looked more futuristic than the more orthodox and chunky layout of the YF-22A. The immediate impression was that the YF-23A

Below: A compromise between performance and stealth, the F-22A was preferred as the Advanced Tactical Fighter over its Northrop rival. Its lines show a weird combination of sleekness and angularity.

Above: The rhombus-shaped front fuselage section of the YF-22A, with just a hint of a chine around it, is to house a phased array radar.

was more stealthy, and possibly faster, while the YF-22A which featured vectoring nozzles, was the more agile and possibly workmanlike. Which would the USAF choose?

The answer came in April 1991, when the YF-22A was selected for further development, to be powered by the Pratt & Whitney F119-100 engine. Eleven flight test F-22s were ordered, with the first scheduled to fly in 1995. It was stated that neither competing aircraft was appreciably more manoeuvrable, faster, or more stealthy than the other, but that Lockheed's programme structure and planning showed greater potential. It was also the cheaper of the two contenders.

The F-22A is slightly larger than the F-15 which it is to replace. The trapezoidal wing is swept back at 48° on the leading edge and forward by 17° on the trailing edge, in a radar-emission deflection measure. The nose is small and pointed, presumably because the active array radar takes up less space than a conventional antenna, and has a distinct chine around it. At the other end, the vectoring nozzles are angled to deflect radar, but they cannot be shielded by the afterbody in the same way as the YF-23A. They are thus more exposed to IR detection, but this was obviously a trade-off, the enhanced agility, and incidentally shorter take-off run, outweighing other considerations. The horizontal tails are mounted on booms outside the line of the engine nozzles, with shape and sweep angles similar to those of the wings. Large trapezoidal twin fin and rudder surfaces are set slightly forward and canted outward at a moderately steep angle. The cockpit transparency is of unorthodox shape, seemingly combining flat areas with sharp curves in an attempt to minimise glint.

The F-22A is reported to handle well, and angles of attack of 60° were reached at an early stage without problems. A supercruise speed of Mach 1.58 was attained during trials, and no problems in separation of gas ingestion were experienced with missile launching from internal bays, which are located on the outside of the engine ducts.

Above: The YF-22A shows its lines to be workmanlike rather than sleek. Roughly the same size as the F-15, it is far more capable.

Above: The steeply canted fins are a stealth measure, but the two-dimensional vectoring engine nozzles can hardly be concealed.

Details of the cockpit layout are sparse, although it is known that multi-function CRT displays are used. Problems have been experienced with high workload on modern fighters. The F-22A will have a system called 'Pilot's Associate' built in, which uses artificial intelligence to monitor systems, situations, and threats, advising the actual pilot on a need to know basis.

The US Navy is in the market for an F-14 replacement in the long term, and is theoretically committed to taking a navalised variant of the ATF. Lockheed have stated that this variant will have a variable geometry wing to improve low speed performance for carrier operations, and more internal fuel. But whether this will ever see the light of day depends, with the reduction of the Soviet threat, as much on budgetary considerations as operational factors.

LTV A-7 Corsair II

A-7D, E, K

Origin: LTV Corporation, Dallas, Texas.
Type: (D, E) Attack aircraft, (K) combat trainer, (L) EW aircraft.
Engines: (D, K) One 14,250lb (6,465kg) thrust Allison TF41-1 turbofan; (E) one 15,000lb (6,804kg) thrust Allison TF41-A-2.
Dimensions: Span 38ft 9in (11.8m), length (D, E) 46ft 1½in (14.06m); (K) 48ft 11½in (14.92m); wing area 375sq ft (34.83m²).
Weights: Empty (D) 19,781lb (8,972kg) (E) 18,942lb (8,592kg); loaded 42,000lb (19,050kg).
Performance: Max speed (D, clean, SL) 599kt (1,110km/hr); (D, 5,000ft/1,524m with 12 Mk 82 bombs) 561kt (1,040km/hr), (E, clean, SL) 602kt (1,115km/hr), (E, 10,000ft/3,048m with 16 Mk 82 bombs) 488kt (904km/hr); initial climb rate (all) 15,000ft/min (76m/sec); service ceiling (all) 42,000ft (12,801m); tactical radius (all) 621nm (1,151km); ferry range (all) 2,484nm (4,604km).
Armament: One 20mm M61A-1 cannon with 1,000 rounds; eight hardpoints rated at 15,000lb (6,804kg); Sidewinder, Walleye Maverick and HARM missiles.
History: First flight (A) 27 September 1965, (D) 26 September 1968, (E) 25 November 1968, (K) January 1981.
User: ANG, USN.

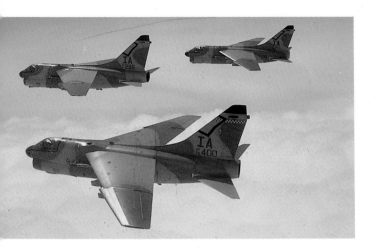

Above: Three A-7D Corsair IIs of the 132nd FW, based at Des Moines, Iowa, formate for the camera. The type is now only used by the ANG.

Below: The A-7E is the USN Corsair variant. This machine is carrying the TALD air-launched decoy on the near pylon.

Development: Like the Phantom, the A-7 Corsair II has operated with all three US air arms, the USAF, USN and USMC. Its parent was the F-8 Crusader, a larger and faster aircraft but one which by the early 1970s was becoming obsolete in USN and USMC service. The A-7 is 8ft 6in (2.6m) shorter than the F-8, and its squat appearance has given rise to a number of affectionate epithets of which SLUF ('Short Little Ugly Fella') and 'Little Hummer' are the best known. It operates as a single-seat, subsonic fighter-bomber, and is capable of delivering a wide range of free-fall or guided ordnance with regularly proven accuracy using a weapon delivery system that works extremely affectively. In South-East Asia the A-7 achieved an outstanding attack capability which has remained with the aircraft ever since and has won for it a number of international bombing competitions in Europe and the USA.

The first of 199 A-7As was delivered to the US Navy in 1966, and the type formed the light attack complement on board US fleet carriers until the arrival of the improved A-7B in 1968. The new variant incorporated a higher-powered engine, and 196 were delivered.

The USAF selected the A-7 to replace the F-100 Super Sabre and ordered 459 of the D variant which was specially tailored to suit the demands of the Air Force's low-level attack requirement. Among the changes incorporated in the D was a higher-powered engine (a licence-built Rolls-Royce Spey, designated Allison T41) and an in-flight refuelling capability to increase loiter time on bombing missions and for ferry flights. The D entered combat over Vietnam on October 1972 and a year later the type was switched from regular TAC squadrons to TAC-assigned units of the Air National Guard. The Corsair II had an extremely accurate nav/attack system, and in 1987, Low Altitude Night Attack (LANA), was fitted to 78 A-7D/Ks. This coupled the TI APQ-126 radar with the flight control system to give terrain following, while a pod-mounted AAR-49 FLIR projected an image onto a wide angle HUD. All remaining Air Force A-7s are now operated by the ANG.

Closely resembling the D model, the A-7E is the Navy's present combat version of the Corsair. It too has a TF41 engine and the same basic avionics, but it incorporates a retractable refuelling probe to match the Navy's drogue system and specialised equipment for carrier operations. The A-7E is primarily used for close air support and anti-shipping missions, and is fitted with FLIR to give night attack capability. The final subtype to enter USN service was the EA-7L

Below: A US Navy A-7E prepares for a catapult launch from its carrier. A FLIR pod can be seen beneath the starboard wing.

EW variant, six of which were converted from two seater TA-7C conversion trainers.

To convert pilots on to the single-seat Corsairs, LTV proposed a two-seat version for the Navy designated TA-7C. Rebuilt from retired A-7As and Cs, the first of 65 examples flew in 1976 and incorporated the second seat in a modified front fuselage. This design proved a success and the USAF followed suit (but considerably later) with the A-7K. Corsairs, both land and carrier-based, flew more than 100,000 sorties in South East Asia, where they acquired an enviable reputation doing everything from close air support to bridge busting. The Lebanon crisis and the invasion of Grenada in 1983 also saw A-7s in action, while USN A-7Es also took part in the Gulf War of 1991, in probably the last actual combat missions of the type.

Below: A USN A-7E prepares for a Gulf War mission, with an AGM-62 Walleye missile underwing. This was the combat swansong of the A-7.

Below: The TA-7C was a two seater conversion trainer for the USN. Highly successful, its USAF two seater equivalent was the A-7K.

McDonnell Douglas A-4 Skyhawk

A-4E, F, M; TA-4F/J; OA-4M

Origin: Douglas Aircraft (division of McDonnell Douglas), USA.

Type: Single-seat attack bomber, (OA) two-seat FAC aircraft, (TA) dual-control trainer.

Engine: (E) One 8,500lb (3,856kg) P&W J52-6 turbojet; (F) 9,300lb (4,218kg) J52-8A, (M) 11,200lb (5,080kg) J52-408A.

Dimensions: Span 27ft 6in (8.38m); length (E, F) 40ft 1½in (12.22m), (M) 40ft 3¼in (12.27m), (OA, TA, exc probe) 42ft 7¼in (12.98m); height 15ft (4.57m), (TA) 15ft 3in (4.65m).

Weights: Empty (E) 9,284lb (4,210kg), (M) 10,465lb (4,747kg), (TA-4F) 10,602lb (4,809kg); max loaded (shipboard) 24,500lb (11,113kg), (land-based) 27,420lb (12,437kg).

Performance: Max speed, loaded (F) 515kt (954km/hr), (M) 560kt (1,038km/hr), (TA-4F) (clean) 586kt (1,086km/hr); initial climb rate (F) 5,620ft/min (28.5m/sec), (M) 8,440ft/min (43m/sec); service ceiling (all, clean) about 49,000ft (14,934m); range (all) about 800nm (1,482km).

Armament: Standard on most versions, two 20mm Mk 12 cannon, each with 200 rounds; pylons under fuselage and wings for total ordnance load of (E, F) 8,200lb (3,720kg), (M) 9,155lb (4,153kg).

History: First flight (XA4D-1) 22 June 1954; (A-4A) 14 August 1954; squadron delivery October 1956, (A-4M) April 1970, (A-4N) June 1972, first of TA series (TA-4E) June 1965, (OA) 1979.

Users: USN, USMC.

Below: Small and versatile, an A-4M 'Camel' Skyhawk of VMA-329 launches a Zuni unguided rocket at a ground target.

Development: Like old soldiers, the US Navy's A-4 Skyhawk force is just fading away, but its memory will never die. The aircraft's capabilities far exceeded its size, and a production run of 2,960 in some seventeen different configurations over 25 years are statistics which will constantly be repeated in connection with this remarkable design.

The brainchild of Douglas designer Ed Heinemann back in 1952, the Skyhawk was the outcome of a US Navy requirement for a carrier-based attack aircraft of 30,000lb (13,600kg) and powered by a turboprop engine. The Douglas team

Above: The Skyhawk could carry a heavy warload for its size, which was such that wing folding to fit carrier lifts was not needed.

97

responded with a 12,000lb (5,440kg) tailed-delta jet bomber with a speed some 100mph (160km/h) faster than specified. Small enough not to need folding wings for carrier stowage, the Skyhawk was ordered by the more than surprised Navy and entered service with VA-62 in October 1956. 'Heinemann's Hot Rod', 'Bantam Bomber' and 'Scooter' became affectionate terms for an aircraft that is easy to fly, maintain and repair.

Although production ended in February 1979, the A-4 remains in Navy Reserve and USMC service. It is no longer operated from the front-line carriers, and most of the Marine-operated single-seaters will be withdrawn when there are sufficient numbers of AV-8B Harrier IIs available.

The A-4E is powered by an 8,500lb (3,855kg) Pratt & Whitney J52-P-6 engine. A total of 498 production Es were built following initial operational status in November 1962 with VA-23. Painted in toned-down grey colours, a number of aircraft fly with Navy units for air combat training, the Skyhawk being similar in performance to the Soviet MiG-17, and the Marines retain some Es in the reserve 4th Marine Air Wing.

The A-4F was the last major single-seat variant developed for the USN. The type has a large dorsal fairing covering additional avionics (hence the nickname 'Camel'), a more powerful 9,300lb (4,220kg) J52 engine, and other modifications. The first of 146 entered service in June 1967.

The A-4M was specially developed for the Marines and 160 aircraft were produced. It has an 11,200lb (5,080kg) thrust J52, a larger canopy, more ammunition for the 20mm guns and a redesigned fin among a number of internal and external modifications.

The TA-4F and J are two-seat models for advanced training. Initially 241 TA-4Fs were built, with deliveries beginning in May 1966 to VA-125 at Lemoore NAS. Most were subsequently converted to J standard, and a further 292 TA-4Js were produced as new-build aircraft. Both types currently equip Navy and Marine advanced and fleet training units. Replacement by the T-45A Goshawk, a navalised version of the British Aerospace Hawk trainer, is now in hand, and TA-4Fs and Js will be phased out completely during the early 'nineties'. The small size and agility of this aircraft makes it well suited to the task, while the fact that it is carrier-compatible is a distinct asset to the Marines, who specialise in amphibious operations.

This small and versatile aircraft is nearing the end of its days with the USN and USMC. It has proved itself in combat in South-East Asia, with the air forces of Israel and Argentina, and by virtue of its simplicity, ruggedness and reliability it will continue to be operated by a number of air arms long after its withdrawal from US service.

Above: TA-4J Skyhawks have seen extensive service in the adversary role, in which they simulate the MiG-17 Fresco. These aircraft are from VA-127 'Cylons', a squadron that flies adversary missions from NAS Lemoore in California, using the tactics and methods of possible hostile air arms. With the dissolution of the Soviet Union, and the increasing obsolescence of the MiG-17 worldwide, the Skyhawk can have little future in the adversary role. Interestingly, the Royal New Zealand Air Force is upgrading its A-4s with improved radar and avionics to a standard 'comparable to the F-16'.

Far Left: The TA-4J remains in USN and USMC service in the advanced training role, although with the service entry of the T-45A Goshawk, its days are numbered, and it will be phased out during the early nineties. This machine has its airbrakes extended.

Left: The very long refuelling probe seen here is typical of the Skyhawk family. This aircraft is a TA-4J of training squadron VT-125. To accommodate the second seat, the fuselage was stretched by 2.5ft (76.2cm) and internal fuel capacity reduced.

99

McDonnell Douglas AH-64 Apache

AH-64A, B, C, D, LONGBOW

Origin: McDonnell Douglas Helicopter Company, Mesa, Arizona.
Type: Attack helicopter.
Engines: Two 1,695shp GE T700-701 free-turbine turboshafts.
Dimensions: Diameter of four-blade rotor 48ft (14.63m); length overall (rotors turning) 58ft 3in (17.76m); span of wings 17ft 2in (5.23m); height overall 16ft 9½in (3.84m); undercarriage track 6ft 8in (2.03m).
Weights: Empty 11,150lb (5,058kg); max loaded 17,650lb (8,006kg).
Performance: Max speed 197kt (365km/hr), max cruise 158kt (293km/hr); max vertical climb 2,530ft/min (13m/sec); max range (internal fuel) 260nm (482km); ferry range 918nm (1,701km).
Armament: One Hughes M230A1 30mm Chain Gun with 1,200 rounds (Honeywell, Aden or DEFA ammunition) in collapsible ventral turret; four wing hardpoints for 16 AGM-114A Hellfire missiles or 76 2.75in (70mm) FFARs in four pods, or mix of these weapons, plus Stinger AAMs.
History: First flight (YAH-64) 30 September 1975; service entry 1985.
User: US Army.

Below: The combination of high performance, extreme agility, and an extensive sensor kit, makes the Apache a formidable opponent.

Above: The nose mounted TADS/PNVS is the heart of the AH-64 Apache's weapons system, comprising FLIR, LLTV, and direct optics.

Development: The AH-64A Apache represents the current production 'state of the art' in helicopter design. Its futuristic shape is no accident nor a designer's whim, but the result of extensive development to produce an attack helicopter for the US Army that can survive combat, is able to take full advantage of NOE (nap of the earth) flight in any weather, day or night, will give its crew the maximum protection possible, and can provide a hefty punch with missiles and guns against enemy tanks.

The basis of the Apache's attack capability is vested in a collection of boxes under the armoured fuselage skin and in the group of strange-looking lumps on the nose. This is the TADS/PNVS, or Target Acquisiton and Designation System/Pilot Night Vision Sensor, produced by Martin-Marietta. TADS includes

Left: Vulnerability to heat-seeking missiles became a problem for helicopters in the early 'eighties. To minimise this, Apache has the 'Black Hole' IR signature suppression unit fitted to the exhaust nozzles, the effluxes of which are canted steeply outwards. The drag penalty is considerable but the engines give sufficient power to ensure that Apache lacks nothing in performance. Other self defence measures include chaff and flare dispensers, RWR, noise reduction measures, and armour that can withstand 23mm hits. With up to 16 AGM-114 Hellfire long range anti-tank missiles and a 30mm Hughes Chain Gun, Apache is formidably armed, and unlike many battlefield helicopters, is fully capable of operating at night.

a low-light-level TV, a forward-looking IR (FLIR) sensor and direct-viewing telescope optics for acquiring the target. There is also a laser rangefinder and a laser target designator to guide the Hellfire anti-armour missiles which form the Apache's main armament. Information from the TADS/PNVS is displayed on the monocle of the Integrated Helmet and Display Sight System (IHADSS). The amazing device permits pilots to view data while watching the target, to point weapons at the target and to cue line-of-sight data between cockpits.

Beneath the front fuselage, in a flexible mounting, is a Hughes-developed 30mm cannon firing standard rounds or specially designed, shaped-charge, chemical-energy, armour-piercing shells. Vital parts of the Apache are protected by armour capable of withstanding hits by 23mm calibre rounds. The flat, non-

Left: The air data sensor mast is clearly seen projecting above the rotor hub in this rear view of an Apache launching two folding fin aircraft rockets at a range target. Rocket pods are an alternative load to Hellfires, for use against close range soft targets.

Below: First flown in September 1975. Apache will be the primary battlefield helicopter for the US Army for many years. Various upgrades are in hand to improve the sensor and weapons systems, but the most important improvement of all would be a significant reduction to its radar signature.

Above: Low over the treetops, an Apache launches a 30mm rocket at a distant target. Smoke like this can give away the Apache's position.

glint cockpit canopy panels are also armoured, and the fuel tanks are self-sealing.

Noise is one of the helicopter's biggest problems, and Hughes engineers have managed to reduce this aspect on the Apache, not quite to 'whisper mode', but certainly to less than that of the current AH-1S Cobra. Hot gases from the engines are dispersed via the company's Black Hole suppression system to reduce significantly the IR signature and protect the machine from heat-seeking SAMs. RWR and flare/chaff dispensers are also fitted for self-defence.

Apache IOC was achieved in July 1986, and it made its combat debut in Panama in December 1989 with a precision strike against General Noriega's Command and Control building. In all, 807 Apaches have been ordered, of which 600 have been delivered by August 1990. In the Gulf War of 1991 it earned a tremendous reputation for its ability to fly and fight at night. Using the long range Hellfire missile with sniper-like accuracy, its crews were able to stand off and shoot while remaining undetected by the Iraqis.

Above: Seen here in Saudi Arabia, Apaches earned a tremendous reputation during the Gulf War of 1991, especially at night.

Above: The Longbow millimetric wave radar is mast-mounted above the rotor hub. MW will replace laser guidance on Hellfire missiles.

Though more advanced that any other battlefield helicopter, Apache's weapons system can still be degraded by rain, fog or smoke. The answer to this is Longbow, a millimetric wave (MW) radar detection and missile guidance system with an antenna mounted in a housing above the rotor head, coupled with Hellfire missiles with MW seekers instead of laser homing. A further Longbow enhancement is the 'MANPRINT' cockpit, featuring two CRTs.

In October 1991, the US Army proposed a fleet modernisation plan for Apache. In this 254 AH-64As would be upgraded to B standard with improved communications and navigation capability, and greater reliability. 308 AH-64As would be converted to C configuration, with more powerful GE T700-701C turboshafts rated at 1,800shp each, MANPRINT crew stations, provision for Longbow plus the MW seeker Hellfire missile. Delivery is scheduled to commence in 1995. Finally 227 AH-64As were to be upgraded to full AH-64D Longbow status, with deliveries scheduled for 1996.

McDonnell Douglas AV-8B Harrier II

AV-8B, TAV-8B, Harrier II Plus

Origin: McDonnell Douglas Corporation, St. Louis, Missouri/British Aerospace, Kingston-upon-Thames, Surrey.

Type: Single seat STOVL close air support fighter.

Engine: (B) One 21,750lb (9,866kg) Rolls Royce F402-406 vectored thrust turbofan, (Plus) one 23,400lb (10,614kg) Rolls Royce F402-408.

Dimensions: Span (All) 30ft 4in (9.24m); length (B) 46ft 4in (14.12m), (Plus) 47ft 9in (14.55m), height (all) 11ft 8in (3.55m), wing area (all) 230sq.ft (21.37m²).

Weights: Empty (B) 13,086lb (5,936kg), (Plus) 14,568lb (6,608kg); max VTO (B) 18,950lb (8,595kg), (Plus) c20,000lb (9,027kg); max TO (all) 31,000lb (14,061kg).

Performance: Max speed S/L (B) 570kt (1,056km/hr), (Plus) 602kt (1,115km/hr); initial climb rate (all) 50,000ft/min (254m/sec); service ceiling (all) 50,000ft (15,239m); operational radius (B) 400nm (741km), (Plus) 450nm (834km).

Armament: (All) one 25mm GAU-12/U five barrel cannon with 300 rounds; (B) six underwing and one ventral hardpoints for a maximum load of 9,260lb (4,200kg) including Sidewinder, Hellfire and Maverick missiles; (Plus) air-to-air, up to six AIM-120A Amraam or a combination of Amraam and AIM-9 Sidewinder.

History: First flight (YAV-8B) 9 November 1978, (FSD AV-8B) 5 November 1981; service entry 1983, Night Attack Harrier September 1989, Harrier II Plus, 1993.

User: USMC.

Right: An AV-8B Harrier II displays its 25mm GAU-12/U cannon pod (left) and ammunition pod (right), joined by a linkless feed.

Below: With two large underwing fuel tanks, a Marine Corps AV-8B does a short rolling take-off from a commando assault ship.

Development: Since it first received the AV-8A Harrier, the US Marine Corps has consistently championed the cause of VTOL aircraft for the support of ground forces. Therefore, despite the relatively high attrition rate of the early aircraft, it came as no great surprise when the Corps announced its intention to order the much-developed AV-8B Harrier II. Preliminary studies were made in the mid-1970s, and the prototype YAV-8B made its first flight from St Louis in November 1978. The prime contractor for the project is McDonnell Douglas, who forged a partnership with British Aerospace back in 1969 which has also seen the recent development and selection of the BAe Hawk (T-45) advanced trainer for the US Navy.

Superficially similar to the AV-8A, the Harrier II 'Marine Machine' is a technically more advanced design and, in the close-support role for which it is intended, it has demonstrated a payload/range capability over 100 per cent better than the earlier aircraft. This is all the more remarkable when it is realised that the basic engine power remains as before. The reason is a combination of factors, but principally that weight has been reduced by the extensive use of composite materials without sacrificing strength. Areas where graphite/epoxy has been used include the forward fuselage, wing, flaps, rudder, fairings and doors, adding up to 26 per cent of the total weight for a saving of 480lb (218kg).

Aerodynamically, the B has a larger, supercritical wing with improved lift devices and leading-edge root extensions for increased manoeuvrability. The bigger wing gives more fuel space, putting overall capacity up by 50 per cent. A more efficient air intake design has been incorporated and better airflow characteristics around the wing have been achieved by altering the vectored thrust nozzles and their position relative to the wing.

The pilot has a better view from the raised cockpit and blown canopy, and an all-new avionics suite reduces the pilot's workload and allows for more accurate weapons delivery. The Harrier II is also the first production combat jet to be equipped with fibre optics communications in place of copper/electrical conductors, the advantages being that optics are immune to electromagnetic interference and proof against external jamming.

The USMC has ordered 328 Harrier IIs, of which 28 are two seater TAV-8B trainers. Delivery of pre-production AV-8Bs began in January 1984, the first unit to receive the type being VMAT-203 at Cherry Point, North Carolina. Since then

Below: The laser seeker/designator in the nose has recently been combined with the carriage of Hellfire anti-tank missiles.

Above: A Harrier II kicks up a cloud of dust and debris as it settles into a clearing among trees. Ground erosion is a problem.

Below: The STOVL ability of the Harrier II simplifies operation in conditions of low visibility and decks made slippery with snow and ice.

Above: The Night Attack Harrier is equipped with a FLIR sensor supplemented by the pilot wearing night vision goggles (NVGs).

the type has been replacing ageing A-4 Skyhawks, and the less capable and more 'twitchy' AV-8Cs, the survivors of which have gone into storage.

The flexibility of STOVL means that the aircraft can fly from large or small ships in support of amphibious landings, transferring to secure forward sites ashore for shorter-range strikes against enemy positions. If caught by enemy fighters, the Harrier II can defend itself with AIM-9 Sidewinder missiles and its single 25mm cannon, but 'viffing' is its one big advantage over conventional aircraft. Using VIFF (Vectoring In Forward Flight), the Harrier pilot can decelerate quickly to force an enemy to overshoot, making him vulnerable to attack from an unexpected quarter.

War does not cease at sunset, and in 1984 McDonnell Douglas were awarded a contract for the Night Attack Harrier. The prototype first flew on 26 June 1987. The first production aircraft entered service on 15 September 1989, and all subsequent Harrier IIs are to this standard. They combine a FLIR sensor and night vision goggles with upgraded cockpit displays, while aircraft delivered from mid-1990 have the more powerful -408 turbofan.

One thing that all AV-8s had lacked was an optimised air combat system. The carriage of Sidewinders went some way towards correcting this deficiency, but gave no medium range capability. The answer was the Harrier II Plus, equipped with the Hughes APG-65 multi-mode radar as used by the F/A-18, also in USMC service. A development contract was awarded to McDonnell Douglas late in 1990, and 24 Plus models were ordered for the USMC. At the same time, there is a high probability that some or all AV-8Bs may be upgraded to Harrier II Plus standard.

Below: The prototype Night Attack Harrier is seen here loaded with two AGM-65 Mavericks and Mk 82 Snakeye retarded bombs.

McDonnell Douglas F-4 Phantom II

F-4E, G, S, RF-4C

Origin: McDonnell Aircraft Company, St Louis, Missouri.

Type: (E, S) multi-role fighter, (G) Wild Weasel defence suppression aircraft, (RF) reconnaissance aircraft.

Engines: (E, G) two 17,900lb (8,119kg) GE J79-17 afterburning turbojets, (RF) two 17,000lb (7,711kg) GE79-15, (S) two 17,900lb (8,119kg) J79-10.

Dimensions: Span (all) 38ft 5in (11.7m); length (E, G) 63ft (19.2m); (RF) 62ft 11in (19.2m); (S) 58ft 2in (17.7m); height (all) 16ft 3in (4.95m); wing area (all) 530sq.ft (49.26m²).

Weights: Empty (E) 29,535lb (13,397kg), (G) 31,000lb (14,062kg), (S) 28,000lb (12,701kg), (RF) 29,292lb (13,287kg); max loaded (E, G) 61,795lb (28,030kg); (S, RF) 58,000lb (26,309kg).

Performance: (All) max speed clean Mach 2.2 at altitude, Mach 1.19 at sea level; initial climb rate 28,000ft/min (142m/sec); service ceiling 55,000ft (16.763m); take-off roll 3,300ft (1,006m); landing roll 3,100ft (945m); combat radius c500nm (927km).

Armament: (E, S) typically four AIM-7 Sparrow and four AIM-9 Sidewinder missiles or variety of air-to-surface ordnance; (E only) one 20mm M61-A1 Vulcan cannon with 640 rounds; (G) four HARM or Standard anti-radiation missiles; (RF) none.

History: First flight (F4H-1) 27 May 1958, (RF) 8 August 1963, (E) 7 August 1965, (G) 6 December 1975, (S) 22 July 1977.

Users: ACC, USAFE, ANG, USMC.

Development: The F-4 Phantom II will surely rank as one of the classic fighters of all time. With its upturned wingtips, anhedral tailplane and aggressively downturned nose, the design stood at the forefront of fighter development in the 1960s. The prototype F4H-1 made its first flight in US Navy colours in 1958 and eventually became the standard front-line fighter aircraft in all three US

Below: This F-4E Phantom II is loaded with two Rockwell GBU-15 glide bombs which give a precision stand-off attack capability.

Services; it was also exported to eleven overseas air forces. It has been estimated that of the 5,173 Phantoms built, some 1,500 will still be in use by the year 2000. As it was originally designed for carrier operations, it was to the US Navy that the first F4Hs — later designated F-4s — were delivered in December 1960; the initial production version, following 24 F-4As, was the F-4B, with 637 aircraft built, and 46 RF-4B reconnaissance versions were produced for the US Marine Corps. In all, 1,218 F-4 fighters were delivered to the USN and USMC and at the peak of their service they equipped 65 squadrons.

In the US Air Force, the Phantom provided the ascendancy needed for air combat in Vietnam, but today only about 600 remain in service, of which 100 are F-4G Wild Weasels and 200 are RF-4Cs, and their numbers are diminishing rapidly as they are replaced by F-15s and 16s. Initially a total of 583 F-4Cs and 793 attack-optimised F-4Ds entered USAF service, but the survivors of these have all been phased out.

The Phantom was seen as an ideal platform for a multi-sensor reconnaissance system aimed at replacing the RF-101 Voodoo in the tactical role. Designated RF-4C, this sophisticated machine carries cameras in a lengthened nose, IR linescan, SLAR (side-looking airborne radar), a mapping radar, a flash/flare cartridge ejection system and ECM/HF equipment. Twenty-four aircraft were given a TEREC (Tactical Electronic Reconnaissance) sensor for locating electronic emitters, while other improvements included the provision of Pave Tack to enhance target location by day or by night and a data link to relay SLAR and TEREC information immediately to battlefield commanders. Less than half the original 505 RF-4Cs remain in service and the Gulf War was probably the combat swansong of the type.

The F-4E was the result of Vietnam experience and incorporated an M61 gun under the nose, an extra fuel cell in the rear fuselage, a new APQ-120 solid-state radar at the front and more powerful J79 engines to cope with the increased weight. All Es were subsequently fitted with leading-edge slats to improve manoeuvrability in combat, and some received TISEO (Target-Identification System Electro-Optical) equipment to aid visual identification of targets at long-range (the system is located on the leading edge of the port wing). Pave Tack and Pave Spike are additional improvements: the former is an all-weather, day or night target designator for IR, laser or EO-guided weapons, whilst the latter is a laser designator pod for daylight use with 'smart' weapons. The 4th TFW

Below: These RF-4Cs of the 67th RW based at Bergstrom AFB, show the lengthened nose with cameras, IRLS and SLAR sensors.

Above: Four F-4G Wild Weasels of the 37th FW at George AFB parade for the camera with a mixed load of HARMs, Mavericks and CBUs.

was the final USAF wing to operate the F-4E. Its last Phantom sortie was flown on 28 December 1990, leaving the ANG as the only remaining US operator.

During the Vietnam War, Wild Weasel was a name synonymous with the SAM-suppression F-105 Thunderchiefs. Their successors are the F-4G Advanced Wild Weasels, the most expensive of all the Phantom variants. Located in and around a standard F-4E airframe are no fewer than 52 aerials designed to detect, identify and locate enemy radars. The main external features of the G are the pods facing forward under the nose and to the rear at the top of the fin.

The Wild Weasel F-4G should not be confused with an earlier F-4G, which was a Navy F-4B with an automatic carrier landing system. A dozen of these were built in 1963 but they were later converted back to B configuration, leaving the G suffix free for reuse some 12 years later. The role of the Weasel is to locate enemy gun and missile radars and destroy them with missiles which home on the radar emissions. Current practice is for F-4Gs to operate in hunter/killer teams with F-16s. The F-4G played an important part in the Gulf

Above: The Weasel Birds gave sterling service during the Gulf War. Carrying two HARMs, this example tanks up over the Saudi desert.

War in suppressing Iraqi air defence systems, and must be credited with saving many allied aircraft.

The US Navy and Marine Corps F-4B was gradually supplanted by the F-4J, the prototype of which first flew on 4 June 1965. This featured more powerful engines, increased fuel capacity, the AWG-10 fire control system, and considerable structural strengthening including Air Force type wide wheels to make it more suitable for operation from land bases. Of the 522 Js built, 302 were further modified to S standard from July 1977. This mainly involved a rebuild to extend service life, plus the addition of new avionics equipment. A handful of F-4Ss remain in service with the USMC as at January 1992.

Many further Phantom updates were proposed for US service. These included the F-4T air superiority fighter, the F-4 (FVS) variable geometry Phantom, and the Boeing/Pratt & Whitney Super Phantom with PW1120 engines, a ventral conformal fuel tank, and upgraded weapons systems and avionics, but these came to nought.

McDonnell Douglas F-15 Eagle

F-15A, B, C, D, E

Origin: McDonnell Douglas Aircraft Company, St. Louis, Missouri.
Type: (A-D) air superiority fighter (E) dual-role interdictor.
Engines: Two afterburning turbofans (A, B) 23,830lb (10,809kg) P&W
F100-100, (C, D, E) 23,450lb (10,637kg) F100-220.
Dimensions: (All) span 42ft 9¾in (13.05m) length 63ft 9in (19.43m), height
18ft 5½in (5.63m), wing area 608sq.ft (56.5m²).
Weights: Empty (A) 28,000lb (12,700kg), (C) 30,300lb (13,744kg), (E)
32,000lb (14,515kg); max take-off (A) 56,500lb (25,628kg) (C) 68,000lb
(30,844kg), (E) 81,000lb (36,742kg).
Performance: (Clean, all) max speed Mach 2.5 at altitude, Mach 1.2 at sea
level, initial climb rate 50,000ft/min (254m/sec), service ceiling 65,000ft
(19,810m); combat radius (loaded) (A) c400nm (741km), (C) 500nm (927km),
(E) 685nm (1,269km). . .
Armament: (All) one 20mm M61A-1 cannon, four AIM-7 Sparrows and
four AIM-9 Sidewinders, later eight AIM-120 Amraam; max external load
(A) 16,000lb (7,258kg), (C) 12,730lb (5,774kg), (E) 24,000lb (10,885kg).
History: First flights (A) 27 July 1972, (B) July 1973, (C) February 1979, (E)
July 1980.
Users: ACC (USAF).

Development: Designed totally for the interception and air superiority missions,
with, as the slogan of the time went 'not a pound for air to ground', the F-15
Eagle remains the most potent fighter in the world in the mid 1990s, some twenty
years after its first flight.

**Above right: Nose-on, an F-15 displays the so-called 'nodding' engine
intakes which move up or down to maintain the optimum rate of
airflow to the engines and thus obtain the necessary efficiency for the
various flight regimes.**

**Right: An F-15A of the 33rd FW, based at Eglin AFB, Florida. This view
emphasises the various major components that form the design, the
two long intake/engine trunks, front fuselage, wings, tailplanes and
fins. Under the fuselage is a 600gal (2,270l) fuel tank.**

**Below: A formation take-off by two F-15As of the 48th FIS based at
Langley. The fintip fairings house radar warning aerials (port) and ECM
aerials (starboard). Arguably still the world's greatest air superiority
fighter, the design is now some 20 years old.**

Above: Dramatically posed against a backdrop of Alaskan mountains and glaciers, this F-15C carriers four AIM-7Fs and four AIM-9Ls.

Optimisation for performance and manoeuvrability resulted in the startling thrust/weight ratio of 1.15 at normal take-off weight in the fighter configuration. Combined with the modest wing loading of 68lb/sq.ft (333kg/m²), this gave an unsurpassed level of performance and a high degree of agility. The Hughes APG-63 multi-mode radar was state of the art for its time, and the cockpit introduced the HOTAS (hands on throttle and stick) concept, whereby all controls needed during critical flight phases, such as combat or landing, are immediately to hand. This is particularly important for a single seater, because the pilot has to operate the radar and weapons systems as well as fly the aircraft, unlike the Eagle's predecessor, the Phantom, which had a second crewman to share the workload. Another first was the use of 'nodding' engine intakes, which adjust automatically to suit the angle of attack. In spite of the 'uncompromised' air superiority role it was inevitable that air-to-ground weaponry would be carried, and this was in fact done from an early stage.

Early Eagles were not without problems. The big Pratt & Whitney turbofans were sensitive to disturbed airflow, and had to be handled with care in order to avoid compressor stalls, while the afterburner sometimes refused to light. In practice the fuel fraction of 0.28 was found to be inadequate, and while this could be compensated by carrying drop tanks, these incurred a performance

Below: Trailing fire and smoke, an AIM-7 Sparrow drops away from this Eagle at launch. Sparrows accounted for many Gulf War kills.

Above: An F-15C pulls in close behind a tanker to top up. In-flight refuelling allows non-stop transatlantic deployments to be made.

Top: Conformal Fuel Tanks, most unusually seen here unfitted. These are a low drag solution to the perennial problem of extra fuel.

Above: The more traditional solution for extra fuel is wing tanks as here, but these cause extra drag, and sterilize weapons stations.

penalty. The F-15A and B were duly replaced on the production lines by the C and D models from June 1979.

The F-15C and D carried an extra 1,820lb (826kg) of fuel internally, and the APG-63 radar was given a programmable signal processor (PSP), which by using software rather than circuitry, gives greater target discrimination and operational versatility. F100-220 turbofans were installed, which are less sensitive and more reliable, although of slightly lower thrust. The C/D was also modified to carry Conformal Fuel Tanks (CFTs) along the fuselage sides. These carry an extra 9,750lb (4,423kg) of internal fuel while having a marginal effect on drag, unlike drop tanks. Another advantage over drop tanks is that they leave free all stores pylons to carry ordnance. Sparrow AAMs are normally carried semi-conformally in tandem pairs on the outside angles of the engine nacelles, but when CFTs are carried these are simply moved to the corresponding position on the tanks. Stub pylons on the CFTs allow the tangential carriage of six pairs of bombs in this position, displacing the Sparrows.

The extra fuel weight, and increased ordnance load has led to higher take-off weights, so another difference between the A and C models is a beefed up undercarriage, wheels and brakes. While it was never officially stated, this creeping weight growth obviously had an adverse effect on performance, as wing loading increased and t/w ratio fell.

Other modifications came under a Multi-Staged Improvement Program (MSIP), commencing in 1985. They include the Hughes APG-70 radar which uses Very High Speed Integrated Circuits (VHSIC) which treble the processing speed, while the aircraft central computer can store four times the amount of data. A new tactical electronic system includes RWR, EW warning and enhanced internal countermeasures. Finally, performance degradation by creeping weight growth has been checked by the installation since 1989 of the more powerful P&W F100-229 or GE F110-229, both rated at about 29,000lb (13,154kg) thrust.

In the early 'eighties, a requirement was formulated for an aircraft to supplement the F-111 in the night and adverse weather deep penetration role. In March 1984 the decision was finally made, and a variant of the F-15, the Strike Eagle as it was then called, was selected. Now better known as the F-15E, the interdictor variant has two crew, with a Weapons Systems Operator (WSO) in the back

Below: The F-15E, seen here loaded with Sparrow and Sidewinder AAMs, Mk82 slicks, and a LANTIRN pod, is a two seater with a Weapons Systems Officer in the back to handle the magic. A much beefed-up variant with an enormous maximum take-off weight, it is primarily an interdictor, but can double in the air superiority role.

seat. As a secondary function, the F-15E supplements the C/D model in the air defence and air superiority roles.

The F-15 has built up a remarkable combat record over the years, at first solely in Israeli service. Four MiG-21s were shot down over southern Lebanon in June 1979, followed by two MiG-25s in 1981. The Beka'a Valley action in June 1982 saw a further 42 Syrian aircraft fall to Israeli Eagles, and a third Foxbat was downed in August of that year. Next blood went to Saudi Arabian F-15s in June 1984, knocking down two Iranian F-4s. In October 1985, Israeli F-15s carried out a long range strike against PLO HQ in Tunis; a round trip of about 2,600nm (4,800km) with the aid of flight refuelling.

First USAF combat came in the Gulf War of 1991, when 120 F-15C/Ds and 48 F-15Es were deployed, flying more than 5,900 and 2,200 sorties respectively. In air combat, USAF F-15Cs accounted for 35 Iraqi aircraft, including five MiG-29s and two MiG-25s, while a Saudi F-15C shot down two Mirage F.1s. The 'Es' were heavily engaged in interdiction and precision attacks, and one actually managed to knock down an Iraqi helicopter with a GBU-10; a most enterprising feat. No F-15s have been lost in air combat, but two F-15Es fell to ground fire during Desert Storm.

Below: F-15Cs of the 36th FW, normally based at Bitburg, are seen loaded for a long range mission over Iraq during the Gulf War.

Above: F-15Cs stand on their Saudi Arabian base in 1991. This type accounted for the majority of air-to-air kills during the conflict.

McDonnell Douglas F/A-18 Hornet

F/A-18A, B, C, D, RC

Origin: McDonnell Douglas Corporation, St Louis, Missouri.
Type: Single- and two-seat multi-mission strike fighter.
Engines: Two 16,000lb (7,257kg) thrust GE F404-400 augmented turbofans.
Dimensions: Span 37ft 6in (11.43m), length 56ft (17.07m), height 15ft 3½in (4.66m), wing area 400sq.ft (37.17m²).
Weights: Empty (A) 21,830lb (9,902kg), (C) 23,000lb (10,433kg); take-off, fighter mission (A) 35,800lb (16,240kg), (C) 36,970lb (16,769kg); max take-off (all) 51,900lb (23,542kg).
Performance: (All) Max speed Mach 1.7, initial climb rate 50,000ft/min (254m/sec), service ceiling 50,000ft (15,239m), combat radius (fighter mission) 405nm (751km), (attack mission) 575nm (1,066km).
Armament: One 20mm M61A-1 multi-barrel cannon with 570 rounds, fighter mission typically four AIM-7 and two AIM-9 (C, D) provision for up to six Amraam; attack mission FLIR and LST/SCAM pods displace two Sparrows; ASMs carried include HARM, Maverick and Harpoon, Paveway LGBs and a variety of conventional ordnance.
History: First flight 18 November 1978, (C) 3 September 1987, (Night Attack D) 6 May 1988.
Users: USN, USMC.

Development: If nothing else, the F/A-18 Hornet can be considered a survivor — not from wartime combat, but from a lobby of antagonists in Congress and in the services who have levelled strong criticism at the aircraft over a variety

Right: F/A-18A Hornets of evaluation squadron VX-5 'Vampires', are seen aboard *USS Constellation* during early carrier trials.

Below: Unusually, the 20mm cannon of the Hornet is mounted on the centreline above the nose. The muzzle orifice is just visible here.

of points ranging from cost overruns to performance shortfalls. The Hornet has indeed had its share of technical problems, which have prompted changes and modifications, but the basic design has weathered a stormy passage from first flight to service introduction.

The origins of the Hornet go back to the early 1970s and the Northrop YF-17 programme. A navalised version was submitted to the US Navy in 1974 in response to a VFAX requirement for a lightweight multi-mission fighter. In refined form the Navy ordered the design and it was agreed that McDonnell Douglas should take over the programme as they had more experience in building naval aircraft.

Production of the F/A-18 was centred on McDonnell's plant at St Louis, with General Electric supplying the smokeless F404 turbofan engines, Hughes the advanced APG-65 long-range look-up/look-down radar, and Northrop providing major portions of the airframe as the principal subcontractor.

Following the first flight of the prototype Hornet, an exhaustive test programme showed up a number of design problems with the aircraft. Modifications involved a redesign of the wing and lateral control surfaces to improve the roll rate at high subsonic speeds and reduce drag, a slight re-shaping of the horizontal stabilisers, and changes to the LEX (leading edge extensions) along the fuselage. As if these problems were not enough, early service experience revealed a weakness in the vertical tails produced by unanticipated stress from high angles of attack. Local reinforcing proved to be inadequate, and the final solution, adopted in the late 'eighties, was to bolt a small metal flange on the upper surface of the LEX. This had the effect of modifying the airflow and reducing the stresses on the fins at high angles of attack.

The Hornet was cleared for the fighter mission by the Naval Air Test Center at Patuxent River by the end of 1981. Clearance for the attack role, however, was withheld after problems were found during trials by the Navy operational evaluation unit in 1982. Much of the criticism centred around the Hornet's ability

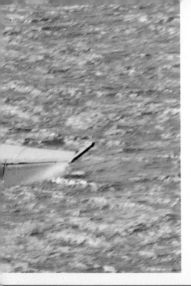

Left: The thrust/weight ratio of the Hornet is sufficient at light weights for take-off without using afterburner, as demonstrated by this aircraft of VMFA-323 'Death Rattlers', as it departs USS *Coral Sea*. The huge flap area and the steeply canted vertical tail surfaces are clearly seen here.

Below: Normal air-to-air armament consists of two AIM-7 Sparrows carried semi-conformally on the fuselage and two AIM-9 Sidewinders on wingtip rails. A Sidewinder is seen being launched from the right wingtip rail of this Marine Hornet of VMFA-314.

to fly attack profiles within its specified 550nm (926km) range with a warload of four 1,000lb (454kg) bombs, FLIR and laser pods and two AIM-9 Sidewinders. Fuel capacity at maximum landing weight was also said to be "modest", a claim contested by the acceptable figures produced during company trials.

On the other hand, the Marines found the Hornet to be just what they wanted to replace the A-7E Corsair. Marine Air Group 11 at El Toro, California, began initial evaluation early in 1983 and produced encouraging combat performance data which showed that, far from being inferior to the A-7 as some had said, the Hornet was much better in most flight regimes than the older aircraft. The pilots found the Hornet to be a superb flying and fighting machine, well able to look after itself in a target area.

Once established, the Hornet soon demonstrated reliability significantly better than any other type in USN service, while it is statistically the safest tactical carrier aircraft ever. Attrition was just 22 aircraft in the first 500,000 flight hours;

Above: A Hornet of VFA-113 'Stingers' releases two Mk 82 slicks in a shallow dive over the Leach Lake weapons range in California.

less than half the figure for the Tomcat. On 10 April 1990, a VFA-136 Knighthawks F/A-18 clocked up the millionth flight hour for the type.

To train Navy and USMC aircrew on the F/A-18, VFA-125 was established at Lemoore NAS, the first deliveries of F-18As and TF-18As being made in 1981. Flying aircraft marked with Navy insignia on one side and Marines on the other, VFA-125 trained pilots for VMFA-314 (the Marines' oldest fighter squadron) and -323, both home-based at El Toro and initially assigned to the carrier *Coral Sea*, and VMFA-531, also at El Toro. The first Navy unit was VFA-113, which relinquished its A-7Es in mid-1983 and operated as part of CVW-14 aboard *Constellation*.

The F/A-18C entered service late in 1987. It differs from the A/B model primarily in the avionics fit, with a high speed mission computer, the ALQ-165 jammer carried internally, and other equipment. A new ACES ejection seat is fitted, and the C model is equipped to carry six AIM-120A Amraam, giving the Hornet a multiple-target engagement facility for the first time.

The next upgrade was the addition of the AAR-50 Thermal Imaging Navigation Set (TINS). This is a pod mounted FLIR with a more limited field of view than Lantirn carried by the F-15E, and has to be supplemented by night vision goggles.

The two seater F/A-18B and D models are fully combat capable, and the reduction in internal fuel to make space for the second seat is only 600lb (272kg). These are traditionally used for pilot training in the USN, but in a departure from tradition, USMC F/A-18Ds are configured for a systems officer, in order to allow the type to replace the elderly A-6E in the night and all-weather interdiction role.

Below: The F/A-18 was designed as a true multi-role aircraft, able to switch from air superiority to bomb truck very quickly.

Other improvements are in the pipeline. From August 1991, new build Hornets will have F404-GE-402 turbofans, giving up to 20 percent more thrust at high speeds and altitudes, while the APG-65 radar is finally to be upgraded, scheduled for service entry in 1994. Another area to be resolved after many years is a reconnaissance Hornet. In 1990, the USMC began to take delivery of the first of 31 F/A-18Ds which have been wired to take a sensor pack in a modified nose section. The sensor pack is scheduled to enter service in 1994 when these aircraft will be redesignated F/A-18RCs.

The Hornet's baptism of fire came in 1986, when several Libyan patrol boats were sunk during Operation Prairie Fire. This was followed a short while later by Eldorado Canyon, the strike against the Libyan mainland, in which Hornet units flew CAP and defence suppression missions. The big one however, was the Gulf War of 1991, in which about 130 USN and USMC Hornets, mainly A/B models, took part. The highlight came on the second day, when two F/A-18Cs of VFA-81 took time out to shoot down two Iraqi MiG-21s before completing their attack mission, thus triumphantly vindicating their dual role capability in a startlingly effective manner.

Right: The anti-shipping mission is an obvious need for a carrier fighter; for this the Hornet carries two AGM-84A Harpoon ASMs. The Hornet's APG-65 radar provides a target update before launch after which the missile is totally autonomous

Above: An early attempt at producing a reconnaissance Hornet led to this FSD aircraft modified into an F/A-18RC, with a sensor pallet.

Above: Many Hornet units saw action during the Gulf War. This one carries long range tanks and has its refuelling probe extended.

Northrop B-2A

B-2A

Origin: Northrop B-2 Division, Pico Rivera, California.
Type: Strategic bomber.
Engines: Four 19,000lb (8,618kg) General Electric F118-100 unaugmented turbofans.
Dimensions: Span 172ft (52.42m); length 69ft (21.03m); height 17ft (5.18m); wing area c5,000sq.ft (464.52m²).
Weights: Empty c160,000lb (72,575kg); max take-off 371,330lb (168,434kg).
Performance: Max speed at altitude Mach 0.9, SL Mach 0.75; service ceiling 50,000ft (15,239m); unrefuelled range 7,500nm (13,898km).
Armament: Typically 16 SRAM IIs, AGM-129s or B.83 free fall special weapons; max weapons load 49,317lb (22,370kg); up to 80, 500lb (227kg) Mk 82 bombs or sea mines.
History: First flight July 1989.

Development: The Advanced Technology Bomber (ATB), as it was known for many years, was scheduled to take over the penetration role from Rockwell's B-1B in the middle to late 1990s, freeing that aircraft to supplant the antediluvian

Below: The Northrop B-2A was designed for low observability to enable it to penetrate defended airspace undetected.

B-52 in the stand-off missile carrying role. Whereas the B-1B flies the penetration phase of the mission in the high drag and fuel consuming ultra low level regime, the B-2A was to penetrate at medium/high altitudes, thus maximising range on internal fuel and reducing reliance on in-flight refuelling. Survivability was to be dependent on low observables technology rather than hiding down in the weeds using extensive countermeasures. This technology had already been demonstrated by the Lockheed XST (see Lockheed F-117A), and in June 1981 the decision was taken to proceed with the ATB which would follow the B-1B into service quite quickly. Northrop were awarded a contract for full scale development in November of the same year.

From the outset it was widely rumoured that the ATB would have a flying wing configuration, a story fuelled by the fact that Northrop had a track record of producing bombers with this planform, notably the XB-35 in 1946, and the four jet YB-49 (which incidently was featured in the film War of the Worlds) in 1947. The flying wing configuration has certain advantages in that with no fuselage and tail, there is less drag-producing wetted area, while loads can be distributed evenly across the span to producing a lighter structure. The weight saved, plus better lift/drag ratio can promise greater range than a traditional layout. On the other hand, the tremendous span to length ratio means that roll and yaw inertia is large, while pitch inertia is small, giving potential control problems which could only realistically be overcome by using FBW, which was of course available during the gestation period of the ATB.

Below: The B-2A displays its weird planform, with angles intended to deflect radar emissions and shield engine effluxes.

Meanwhile advances had been made in computer technology which enabled the radar reflectivity of curved surfaces to be predicted (this had not been available for the F-117A), which assisted in producing a stealthy design. The flying wing had advantages in this field also, as the crew, engines, avionics and weapons bays could be sunk in the depth of the centre section with only minimal protuberances, while vertical stabilising and control surfaces, which often form radar reflecting angles, could be eliminated altogether.

A moderate leading edge sweep angle of about 40° was selected, while the centre section, thickened to hold cabin, engines, and weapons bays, was extended aft to give a W shaped trailing edge. This extra length allowed the engine inlets and effluxes to be set above the wing, where they are less vulnerable to both radar and IR detection systems.

An extensive redesign took place in 1984, when the Air Force decided that they wanted the B-2A to be capable of low level penetration as well as high. A sharper sweep angle was investigated to improve gust response and reduce drag, but rejected on several grounds. Vertical fins would have been needed for directional control, range on internal fuel would have been reduced significantly, and afterburning would have been needed at take-off. In the event, the original sweep angle was retained and various bulkheads and other structural members beefed-up to carry the additional spanwise loads at low level. To accommodate these, the cockpit was moved forward and the engine intakes relocated aft. The wing leading edge was modified to improve control, and a new double W trailing edge profile adopted to reduce structural loadings at low level by moving the control centre of pressure.

The first B-2A was rolled out at Palmdale on 22 November 1988, in front of a carefully selected audience. The external shape was very smooth, and made extensive use of radar absorbent composites. First flight took place on 17 July 1989, when the prototype left Palmdale for Edwards AFB where the majority of the flight test programme was carried out.

Control surfaces consist of three sets of elevons on the trailing edge, and split surface drag rudders (which also double as air brakes) outboard. Low wing loading allows short take-off and landing rolls and acceleration is exceptional for an aircraft of its size. It has been stated that the B-2A has certain control problems, and with such a radical layout this is only to be expected, but the quadruplex FBW system 'handles them very nicely'.

In the early days of the project, it was stated that one of the primary missions was to track down and destroy Soviet SS-24 Scalpel and SS-25 Sickle mobile ballistic missiles, but this was later quietly dropped, as the detection technology was lacking. It has since been revealed that the B-2 will be equipped with the Hughes APQ-181 synthetic aperture radar, with 21 modes including target search and detection. On the other hand, the use of active radar will tend to negate the stealthy qualities of the aircraft, rather like a burglar who switches on a torch.

Initially 165 aircraft were planned. This was later reduced to 132, but the diminution of the Soviet threat during 1989-91 has reduced this still further. It is now likely that no more than 15 or 20 B-2As will finally be built.

Below: The unfamiliar lines of the B-2A make it difficult to judge its size. Here a KC-10A Extender tanker gives it scale.

Rockwell B-1 Lancer

B-1B

Origin: Rockwell International, North American Aircraft, El Segundo, California.
Type: Strategic bomber.
Engines: Four GE F101-GE-102 augmented turbofans, each rated at 30,000lb (13,605kg) with full afterburner.
Dimensions: Span (fully spread) 136ft 8½in (41.67m), (fully swept) 78ft 2½in (23.84m); length 147ft (44.8m); height 34ft (10.36m); wing area 1,950sq.ft (181.18m²).
Weights: Empty 180,000lb (81,647kg), max loaded 477,000lb (216,366kg).
Performance: Max speed (altitude) Mach 1.40, sea level Mach 0.85; service ceiling 49,000ft (14,934m); range on internal fuel 6,500nm (12,045km); field length less than 4,500ft (1,372m) at light weights.
Armament: Eight AGM-86B cruise missiles internally plus four externally; 24 AGM-69 SRAM internally plus 14 externally; 24 B61 or B83 special

weapons internally plus 14 externally; 84 500lb (227kg) bombs; Mk 36 or 60 sea mines.
History: First flight (B-1A) 23 December 1974, (B-1B) 18 October 1984, final delivery January 1989.
User: ACC.

Development: When the 96th Bomb Wing at Dyess AFB, Texas, received its first Rockwell B-1B in March 1985 there could have been few members of SAC who did not look on the drab shape and sigh with relief as they remembered President Carter's decision in 1977 to halt the B-1 programme, leaving the ageing B-52 and the none-too-plentiful FB-111 to promote America's manned bomber deterrent. That the B-1 survived and did not go the way of the XB-70 was due to a number of factors, chief among these being the need for a balanced strategic triad (manned bombers, ICBMs and submarine-launched missiles), neglected under Carter but nurtured by President Reagan.

Below: The Rockwell B-1B Lancer was designed for low level penetration of defended airspace at high subsonic speed, using a combination of low observables and sophisticated ECM.

The B-1B is similar in shape to the four B-1A prototypes built in the 1970s, but under the skin it is a very different aeroplane, incorporating technical advances to ensure that it can penetrate modern defences well into the 1990s. Two of the B-1As were used to prove the modifications of the redesign, the second prototype being used for weapons and systems development and the fourth aircraft for defensive and offensive avionics testing.

From the 1970s, increasing attention was given to reducing detectability by radar, and the B-1B benefited considerably from advances made in the field. The inlets were made serpentine and given curved baffles to shield the compressor faces, while the antenna of the terrain-following radar was slanted downwards to deflect enemy radar emissions away at an angle; composites replaced metal in the weapons bay doors, while wing glove seals were of the 'sliding feathers' type pioneered by Tornado. Some 85 locations on the airframe, including the leading and trailing edges of the wings and tail surfaces, have received radar-absorbent coatings; even the sharp angles in the cockpit have been rounded where possible. The result is that the B-1B has an RCS one-hundredth that of the B-52.

The Eaton AN/ALQ-161 programmable defensive avionics system gives 360° coverage. Hostile radar emissions are automatically detected, identified, and assigned priorities. Jamming is then initiated if necessary, the final judgement

Above: The interesting compound curves seen from this angle are part of the attempt to keep the radar cross-section of the B-1B at a much lower value than earlier bombers.

Left: Wings fully swept, a B-1B flies over the Mojave desert. The white markings are an aid to the boom operator of the tanker during inflight refuelling.

Below: The inlets of the B-1B engines are serpentine, with curved baffles. This shields the compressor faces from the prying eyes of hostile radars.

Above: Radar reflective areas of the B-1B are covered with RAM to absorb radar emissions, as with this patch around the ride vane.

being the responsibility of the specialist defensive systems operator. ALQ-161 has been criticised as not meeting performance targets, but it has nearly double the capability of previous systems. Also fitted is the Westinghouse ALQ-153 tail warning radar, but this can obviously only be used when it is known that the B-1B has already been detected.

In the nose is the Westinghouse APQ-164 multi-mode radar, which has a fixed phased array antenna using electronic scanning. At least thirteen modes are available including automatic terrain following, allowing penetration to be made at night at altitudes down to 200ft (60m). Mapping and synthetic aperture modes aid navigational accuracy, in conjunction with INS, TACAN, and lately (GPS) Global Positioning System.

The mission profile of the B-1B is to disperse to small airfields in times of international tension, scramble within four minutes, refuel in mid-air, cruise out at economical altitude and speed, then fly the penetration phase at very low altitude and high subsonic speed to attack with nuclear missiles or bombs. Fortunately it now appears improbable that this mission will ever be flown, although conventional bombing and minelaying sorties cannot be ruled out for the future.

Below: The nose of the B-1B contains the APQ-164 radar, with automatic terrain following, synthetic aperture, and other modes.

Rockwell OV-10 Bronco

OV-10A, D

Origin: Rockwell International, Ohio.
Type: FAC Aircraft.
Engines: Two Garrett turboprops (A) 715ehp T76-416/417, (D) 1,040shp T76-420/421.
Dimensions: Span (all) 40ft (12.19m); length (A) 41ft 7in (12.67m), (D) 44ft (13.41m); height (all) 15ft (4.56m); wing area (all) 291sq.ft (27.03m²).
Weights: Empty (A) 6,893lb (3,127kg), loaded (A) 12,500lb (5,670kg) (D) 14,625lb (6,634kg); overload (A) 14,444lb (6,552kg).
Performance: Max speed (A) 244kt (452km/hr), (D) 260kt (482km/hr) initial climb rate (A) 2,600ft/min (13m/sec), (D) 3,100ft/min (16m/sec); service ceiling (A) 24,000ft (7,315m); (D) 30,000ft (9,144m); take off run (A) 1,740ft (530m), (D) 1,500ft (457m); landing run (A) 740ft (226m), (D) 800ft (244m) combat radius (max weapon load, no loiter) (all) 198nm (367km); ferry range (all) 1,200nm (1,382km).
History: First flight (A) 16 July 1965, (D) 9 June 1970.
Users: ACC, TAC, PACAF, USAFE, USMC.

Development: A number of aircraft currently used by the US forces have their origins in the Vietnam War, a conflict which, under the tough operational rules prevailing, the Americans found to be unwinnable. The North American (later Rockwell) OV-10 Bronco was one design which answered the need for a rugged

counter-insurgency aircraft which could deliver a modest amount of firepower against enemy troops, equipment and strong-points. As it turned out, the USAF modified the Bronco's role and it became a Forward Air Control aircraft, locating, identifying and marking Viet Cong targets for attack by tactical fighters. In this task the Bronco proved ideally suited, so much so that today it continues to operate in the FAC role.

The crew of two sit out in front of the wing and engines in the fuselage nacelle, enjoying a superb field of view, whilst the weapon carriage of up to 3,600lb (1,630kg) is more than adequate to supplement the firepower from the bigger jets. For self-defence, Sidewinder missiles can be carried on the Bronco's outboard underwing pylons. At the rear of the crew nacelle there is accommodation for five troops, two stretcher cases or cargo.

Of the original 157 OV-10As received by the USAF, only about 75 remained in service in early 1992, and these are being phased out in favour of the faster and more survivable OA-10A Thunderbolt II. The USMC acquired 114 Broncos, of which about 66 remain in the inventory. These are all scheduled for conversion to OV-10D configuration, with more powerful engines and night capability with the addition of an AN/AAS-37 FLIR in an extended nose; NVGs, and a reconfigured cockpit with better displays. Provision has been made for these aircraft to have a 20mm cannon mounted in a turret under the nose, plus Sidewinder and Hellfire missiles. A service life extension programme was begun for USMC OV-10Ds in 1988.

Below: Marine OV-10Ds are the only examples of the type to remain in service past 1992, and these will have a FLIR in an extended nose and reconfigured cockpit displays.

Weapons

Every one of the aircraft listed in the preceding pages has a single common purpose, that of bringing weapons to bear on a target. For many years the primary fighter weapon was the gun, but with the advent of guided missiles in the 1950s, it was increasingly regarded as obsolete. Wars in the Middle East and Vietnam soon disproved this notion, and since that time no fighter has been without one; but the increasing capability and reliability of the latest generation of guided missiles has since relegated the gun to a secondary position as a weapon of last resort.

Air-to-air missiles have traditionally fallen into two categories; long and medium range weapons with radar homing, and visual range 'dogfight' missiles which guide on the IR emissions of the target. In the former category, semi-active radar homing was the preferred method, with the parent fighter illuminating the target during the missile time of flight. This is in the process of being supplanted by inertial midcourse guidance, updated at intervals, with active radar or IR terminal homing.

Air-to-surface ordnance is a vast subject, encompassing strategic and tactical, area and precision, guided and unguided, free-fall and propelled weapons, ranging from the cluster bomb to the air launched cruise missile.

Guns

M61A1 Vulcan 20mm cannon

Produced by General Electric, the famous Vulcan six-barrel gun equips most of America's front-line fighters, and has done so for nearly 25 years. It is drum-fed and usually employs linkless ammunition. Maximum rate of fire is 6,600 high-velocity rounds per minute, although no aircraft carries that many shells in normal circumstances. Aircraft using the M61 include the A-7, F-4, F-14, F-15, F-16, F-18, and F-111, whilst the T-171 is the version fitted to the rear remote-controlled position in the B-52H. The podded versions of the Vulcan are designated SUU-16/A and SUU-23/A, which differ in detail but have the same performance.

Below: The most widely used aircraft gun in US service is the 20mm General Electric M61A Vulcan, seen here in SUU-16/A pod form.

GAU-12/U 25mm cannon
Unique to the AV-8B Harrier II, this recent GE-developed gun is fitted in the port ventral pod and fed from the starboard pod which carries 300 rounds of linkless ammunition. A five-barrel weapon, it fires the Bushmaster family of ammunition which includes HE, incendiary and armour-piercing rounds. Rate of fire is approximately 3,600 rounds per minute.

GAU-8/A Avenger 30mm cannon
With a length of 21ft (6.4m) without the magazine drum and a round which is larger than the normal 30mm shell, this gun is the most powerful weapon of its kind now flying. Projecting menacingly from the nose of the A-10A Thunderbolt, the GAU-8/A can fire depleted uranium-cored, armour-piercing rounds at a rate of 2,000 or 4,000 per-minute from its seven barrels. The shells are fed from a large drum in the body of the fuselage via a winding conveyor system, the drum accommodating 1,174 rounds of linkless ammunition.

Below: An A-10A Thunderbolt II trails smoke from its massive 30mm GAU-8/A Avenger cannon. It fires shells with depleted unranium cores.

Below: The seven-barrelled GAU-8/A on display, with its enormous ammunition drum. The unit is as long as the average family car.

145

Air-to-Air Missiles

AIM-7 Sparrow

The AIM-7F is currently the most widely used version of this medium-range, all-weather, semi-active radar guided missile. It has a reach of some 54nm (100km) and has shown itself to be capable of performing well in combat. The latest production variant is the AIM-7M, which has the same external dimensions and appearance as the F but features a monopulse seeker head which provides better performance in natural clutter and ECM. Length 12ft (3.66m); warhead 88lb (40kg).

AIM-9 Sidewinder

Undoubtedly one of the great missile designs of all time, Sidewinder is now in its third decade of service with the US forces. Such is its success that the basic design was copied by the Soviet Union as the K-13, codenamed AA-2 Atoll by the West. AIM-9L is an all aspect weapon, but still works best when launched from the traditional six o'clock position. The L is recognisable by the 'double delta' control fins compared with the triangular shape on earlier versions. The improved-performance AIM-9M is now in production and service. Length (L) 112.2in (2.85m); range 9nm (17.7km).

Below: The standard US medium range air-to-air missile is the AIM-7 Sparrow, seen here on its trolley prior to loading.

Above: The AIM-9 is the most widely used close combat missile in the world. This is the AIM-9L, on the wingtip rail of an F-16.

AIM-54 Phoenix

Developed by Hughes for use with the F-14A Tomcat, the Phoenix has a range of some 80nm (148km) and is a 'fire-and-forget' radar guided missile with mid-course inertial guidance and active radar terminal homing. Using Tomcat's advanced AWG-9 radar, six Phoenix can be fired near-simultaneously against six different targets. The solid fuel motor gives the missile a speed to burnout of Mach 5. The latest variant is the AIM-54C, which has an improved target detecting device and an enhanced ECCM capability. Length 157.8in (4.01m); warhead 132lb (60kg). When Tomcats have been in combat they have used Sparrows and Sidewinders, and the Phoenix remains unproven.

AIM-120 Amraam

The Advanced Medium Range Air-to-Air Missile has been developed to replace Sparrow. The same length as the earlier missile, it has a slightly smaller body diameter (7in/178mm), and at 335lb (152kg) is significantly lighter. Its range is about 40nm (74km), which is rather less, but its all burnt speed is higher, at Mach 5. Inertial midcourse guidance, which can be updated during flight by the launching fighter, is used in conjunction with active radar terminal homing. A 'fire and forget' weapon, which does not need the fighter to continue to close the target, it allows several targets to be engaged simultaneously. It was stated to have been deployed in the Gulf War of 1991, but surprisingly, no kills have been attributed to it.

Above: This F-16 has AIM-9Ms supplemented with two AIM-120 Amraam to give it a credible beyond visual range capability.

Air-to-Ground Weapons (Unpowered)

AGM-62 Walleye

An unpowered glide bomb with TV guidance, Walleye has been produced in three versions — I, II and Extended-Range Data-Link — and is in service with the USAF and US Navy/Marines. Once launched with the missile TV camera locked on to the target, the carrier aircraft can depart from the area leaving the bomb to do the rest. Length (II) 13.2ft (4.04m); range (II) 30nm (56.3km).

Paveway

Paveway laser-guided bombs were first used during the Vietnam War, providing precision weapon delivery against a wide variety of targets. Using as a basis a standard 500lb (225kg), 1,000lb (450kg) or 2,000lb (900kg) 'iron' bomb, Paveway incorporates a guidance head with movable fins. The energy from the laser-illuminated target is reflected and detected by the laser guidance head, which computes appropriate commands to the movable surfaces and thus influences the trajectory of the bomb and steers it to the target. Following the initial Paveway I, the more advanced Paveway II entered service in 1978 with the

Below: A direct hit scored by a Paveway LGB. Laser guidance gives superb accuracy in the right operational conditions.

USAF and US Navy, equipping all the principal attack aircraft. Folding rear wings are also a feature of the II series, which are designated GBU-10 Mk 84 2,000lb (900kg), GBU-12 Mk 82 500lb (225kg), and GBU-16 Mk 83 1,000lb (450kg). Paveway III was developed in 1980-81 and is a version designed for low-altitude delivery and having a modest stand-off capability. Improvements include high-lift folding wings and a better scanning seeker. Texas Instruments produce the laser guidance kit.

GBU-15 Cruciform Wing Weapon

A precision-guided glide bomb, the GBU-15 is in current USAF service and comprises a Mk 84 2,000lb (900kg) general-purpose bomb equipped with a TV-guidance seeker and data link. It is designed for use against targets such as railways, buildings and bridges. The kit can also be fitted to the M118 3,000lb (1,360kg) bomb and the SUU-54 bomblet dispenser, which is designed for operations against larger area targets. A powered version of the GBU-15 designated AGM-130A has been developed by Rockwell International; this has a range of about 13nm (24km) when released at low altitude. A night attack capability is proposed for the future, using an IIR seeker.

Below: The Rockwell GBU-15 is a glide bomb which uses electro-optical guidance with a data link to the controlling aircraft.

Rockeye Mk 20 Cluster Bomb
Developed by the US Navy in the mid-1960s, this 500lb (225kg) weapon releases 247 fragmentation bomblets. A laser-homing version is in service with a KMU-420 guidance package, and a dispenser called APAM (Anti-Personnel/Anti-Material) is in use but with 717 bomblets.

Snakeye Mk 82
The petal airbrakes are a distinctive feature of this high-drag 500lb (225kg) 'iron' bomb; without the retarding system, the weapon becomes a 'slick' low-drag bomb. A laser head can be fitted.

Durandal
This French (Matra-designed) anti-runway weapons system was selected by the USAF in September 1983 and since then many thousands have been delivered for use with tactical aircraft. Low-level release is followed by deployment of a retarding parachute, rocket acceleration and penetration into the runway, with instant detonation or time delay.

CBU-55 Fuel-Air Explosive Weapon
The principle of the FAE weapon is the creation of a cloud of fuel-air mixture which is then detonated to achieve an explosive affect. Both the USAF and the Navy have these weapons in service, in order to clear large areas of mines, booby traps, etc. One example is the CBU-55, which weighs 500lb (225kg) and comprises three canisters of fuel which separate after dropping, to produce a high blast overpressure when ignited.

LAU-32 Rocket Pod
Various types of pods carrying a number of unguided rockets are used by the US forces. The LAU-32 contains 19 rockets and the LAU-10 has three 5in (127mm) Zuni rockets.

Nuclear bombs
There are a number of nuclear bombs in service carried by the main types of tactical and strategic aircraft. The B28 is a free-fall weapon deployed by the B-52 (up to eight), A-6 (three) and B-1B (up to 20), and the B43 is tactical/strategic, retarded or free fall. The B61 is similar to the -43 but has yields in the 100-500kT range; up to 38 can be carried by the B-1B. Nuclear warheads for a range of missiles are given "W" prefixes, for example W72 for Walleye and W80-1 for the head of the AGM-86B ALCM.

Above: Effective against soft area targets, Rockeye CBUs (seen above carried by an F-15E) each contain large numbers of bomblets.

Below: Iron bombs such as these Mk 82 slicks, made up by far the greatest weight of munitions dropped on Iraq during the Gulf War.

Air-to-Ground Missiles

AGM-86B Air-Launched Cruise Missile

The main weapon of the B-52G and B-1B, the ALCM is carried on internal rotary launchers or underwing pylons. Powered by a Williams 600lb (272kg) thrust turbojet, it has a range of up to 1,350nm (2,500km) at high subsonic speed at low altitude, using a combination of inertial navigation and terrain contour matching (Tercom) to find its target, allied to a terrain following system. Its replacement, the AGM-129 Advanced ALCM, is currently under development to arm the Northrop B-2A. This is a totally new missile with the accent on low observables.

AGM-69 Short-Range Attack Missile

SRAM is a supersonic air-to-surface nuclear missile carried by the B-52G/H (20 missiles) and B-1B (38). With a warhead yielding 200kT, SRAM has a range of between 30 and 91nm (56-169km) depending on the attack profile (semi-ballistic, terrain-following, pull-up followed by a dive on target, or combined inertial and terrain-following). A total of 1,500 missiles were built. Length 14ft (4.27m); weight 2,230lb (1,012kg).

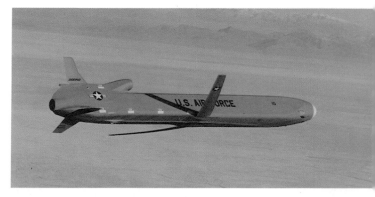

Above: The AGM-86B cruise missile gives a stand-off capability to strategic bombers, allowing attacks to be made from a safe distance.

Below: AGM-84A/D Harpoon is a sea-skimming anti-ship missile with inertial midcourse guidance and active radar terminal homing.

AGM-131A SRAM II

SRAM II, developed by Boeing, is a smaller weapon than AGM-69, being about 14ft (4.27m) long, 15½in (396mm) diameter, and weighing about 2,000lb (907kg). Production began in 1991, but IOC is not scheduled until 1994.

AGM-84A/D Harpoon

Harpoon is an anti-shipping missile which uses a low level approach with inertial guidance, and a terminal pop up and dive attack using active radar homing, to penetrate enemy defences. It is carried by USAF B-52s and B-1Bs as well as USN aircraft. The HE warhead weighs 488lb (221kg), range exceeds 67nm (124km).

AGM-84E Stand-off Land Attack Missile

SLAM combines the airframe and propulsion system of Harpoon with the Hughes IIR seeker of Maverick, the Walleye data link and a GPS receiver for precise midcourse navigation updates. This combination allows precision attacks on high value targets at stand-off ranges of more than 60nm (111km). First operationally used in the Gulf War of 1991.

Above: AGM-84E SLAM is a hybrid missile based on Harpoon, with a Maverick IIR seeker, used for precision attacks at medium range.

Above: AGM-88C HARM is a high speed anti-radiation missile similar in appearance to Sparrow, which is used to destroy hostile radars.

Above: A USN A-6E Intruder is seen here carrying HARM missiles and Mk 82 slicks in the defence suppression role.

AGM-65 Maverick

Variants of this well-proven missile have now reached the G suffix, and the H, using millimetric homing, is currently under development. AGM-65D combines an IIR seeker for night or adverse weather with a shaped charge warhead; E uses laser guidance with a dual role HE warhead; F is an anti-shipping missile with the IIR seeker of the D and large warhead of the E, while G is the USAF equivalent for attacks on hardened targets. Range (all) about 12nm (22km).

AGM-132 Have Nap/Popeye

Popeye is a large and extremely destructive missile designed by Israel, which was evaluated by the USA under the name of *Have Nap*. 16ft 8in (5.08m) long and 21in (56cm) diameter, Popeye weighs 3,000lb (1,361kg) of which no less than one third is the warhead. Guidance is electro-optical, and range is stated to be 50nm (92km). It is known to have been used by B-52s in the Gulf War of 1991, although it can also be carried by tactical aircraft.

AGM-88 High Speed Anti-radiation Missile

HARM is now the standard anti-radar missile of the US services, and played an important part in reducing Iraqi air defences to a state of near impotence

Above: AGM-114A Hellfire is the primary anti-tank weapon of the AH-64A Apache. It is supplemented here by pods of unguided rockets.

in the Gulf War. Recent improvements include a reprogrammable memory allowing new threats to be matched. The latest model is AGM-88C. Range is 10nm (18½km).

AGM-114A Hellfire

The primary weapon of the AH-64 Apache attack helicopter, Hellfire uses semi-active laser guidance and has the long (for an anti-tank missile) range of 3.6nm (6km). A single stage solid rocket motor propels it at 772kt (1,430km/hr), giving it a short time of flight, and its shaped charge warhead can penetrate more than 27½in (70cm) of rolled homogeneous armour. Future Hellfires are expected to use millimetric wave guidance.

BGM-109 TOW

TOW (Tube launched, Optically guided Weapon) has been the primary US helicopter-launched anti-tank missile for many years. It is however fairly old technology, using SACLOS (Semi-Automatic Command to Line Of Sight) guidance in which the operator keeps the sight trained on the target while the computer sends steering commands through trailing wires. Max speed is 641kt (1,188km/hr), and range is 2nm (3¾km). The latest TOW missiles have a double, downwards angled charge for defeating reactive armour in a top attack.

OTHER SUPER-VALUE MILITARY GUIDES IN THIS SERIES

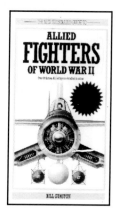

OTHER ILLUSTRATED MILITARY GUIDES AVAILABLE

Modern Tanks & Fighting Vehicles
Modern Rifles & Sub-Machine Guns
Modern Elite Forces
Weapons of the Elite Forces
Modern Warships

★ Each title has 160 fact-filled pages
★ Each is colorfully illustrated with hundreds of action photographs and technical drawings
★ Each contains concisely presented data and accurate descriptions of major international weapons systems
★ Each title represents tremendous value for money